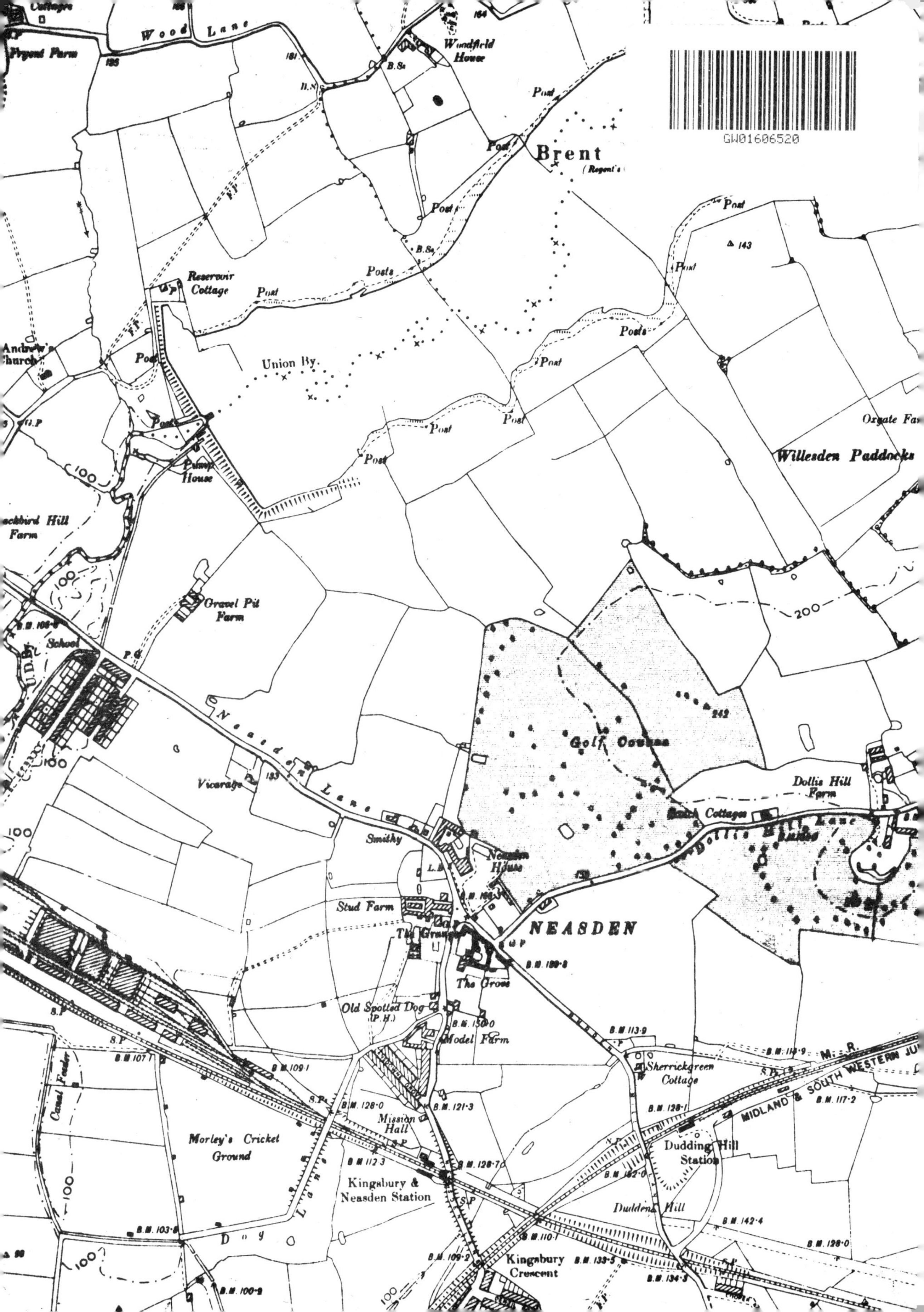
Wood Lane
Woodfield House
Brent
Reservoir Cottage
Union By.
Pump House
Gravel Pit Farm
School
Neasden Lane
Vicarage
Smithy
Neasden House
Golf Course
Dollis Hill Farm
Dollis Hill Lane
Willesden Paddocks
Stud Farm
The Grange
NEASDEN
The Grove
Old Spotted Dog (P.H.)
Model Farm
Sherrickgreen Cottage
Mission Hall
Morley's Cricket Ground
Kingsbury & Neasden Station
Dudding Hill Station
MIDLAND & SOUTH WESTERN JU
Kingsbury Crescent
Dog Lane
Canal Feeder
GW01606520

NEASDEN:

A HISTORICAL STUDY

NEASDEN

A HISTORICAL STUDY

K. J. VALENTINE

CHARLES SKILTON

Made and printed in Great Britain
and published by
CHARLES SKILTON LTD
Whittingehame House
Haddington
East Lothian

ISBN 0284 98662 3

CONTENTS

PART ONE: Before 1800

PART TWO: The Half-Century to 1853

PART THREE: The Prout Era (1853-81)

PART FOUR: The First Transformation

PART FIVE: The Second Stage

PART SIX: The Final Surge

ILLUSTRATIONS

AUTHOR'S PREFACE

FOR this study of Neasden primary sources of evidence have been used wherever possible. Consequently extensive use has been made both of local archives, especially in the library of the Grange Museum at Neasden, and of national and county records at the Public Record Office, the Greater London Record Office, the House of Lords Record Office, etc. Quotations from all Crown copyright records appear by permission of the Controller of H.M. Stationery Office.

The author is also indebted to the British Library, the Guildhall Library and the archivists of many bodies including the Church Commissioners, the Royal Mint, the Goldsmiths Company and the Home of Rest for Horses at Speen.

On a personal level valuable biographical information about the Nicoll/Prout/Nicol family was given to me by Col.J.W.Nicol of Ballogie and by Mr Thomas Stainton of Beaconsfield, while Mr John Roberts of Richmond, Virginia, kindly gave me access to past studies made of his family's history. Finally, I am grateful for assistance from friends who knew pre-1914 Neasden, including Miss Denise Kidson, Mr David Ayerst and Mr Dudley Glanfield.

Permission to publish photographs was kindly given as follows: nos. 3 & 11 by the Greater London Record Office, no. 4 by London Transport, no. 10 by the Leicestershire Record Office and nos. 1, 2, 7, 8, 9, 12, 13 & 14 by the Grange Museum.

Neasden K.J.V.

INTRODUCTION

IN FEBRUARY 1972 'Neasden' was a household word throughout the land. For a decade *Private Eye* had systematically equated it with suburban facelessness; and in the small-talk of smart circles the name excited the same sort of derision that 'Wigan' had done in an earlier age. So when the news got around that Neasden was about to have a modern underpass conferred upon it the *Times* newspaper decided to send out a scout to discover for itself and for its readers what this notoriously insignificant place was really like.

The outcome of this reconnaissance was described in a 700-word article which said that Neasden was a pleasant, unremarkable place and that the 'scoffers' had got it wrong. Dollis Hill and Gladstone and the Welsh Harp were mentioned but there was no hint that Neasden's history might be anything out of the ordinary; indeed, readers were given the impression that the most notable products of the place were the actress Twiggy and Judy Grinham the swimmer. Since then the scoffing has gone on and even in the 1980s was indulged in by a former Cabinet minister on television. The idea persists that Neasden has no history worth talking about; it is time to put the record straight.

What little is known about Neasden's early history is largely contained in accounts about Willesden such as *The Story of Willesden* (1926) by the late Professor Simeon Potter — who himself belonged to Neasden in his boyhood — and volume VII of the *Victoria County History of Middlesex* (1982). But some of what is traditionally said about 17th-century Neasden is incorrect; for instance both the *Dictionary of National Biography* and the *VCH* are wrong about the baronetcy held by the Roberts family at Neasden House. And Neasden's history in the 18th century, and also in the 19th century before the arrival of the railways, is almost unknown.

There is a special reason for this. About a century ago an energetic local politician, F.A. Wood, collected together a huge amount of historical material about Willesden, some of it inevitably fragmentary, but he detested what Neasden stood for in local affairs and did little work on its history. Consequently it has never been told (and has probably not been known in Willesden for a century) how the Nicolls, coming to Neasden early in the 18th century soon after the powerful Roberts family had faded from the scene, quickly established themselves as the leading family of Neasden and later as one of the most influential families of Willesden. Equally unknown is the part this family played for a century in the Company of the Moneyers at the Royal Mint on Tower Hill — when Neasden and other parts of north Willesden were quite literally 'in the money'. By the 1870s almost all of the land at Neasden belonged to the Nicoll family in the persons of Catherine Prout and her father John. After John's death in 1881 Catherine and her husband, who lived in Kensington, acted most generously towards the new parish of Neasden-cum-Kingsbury and though both died soon after war broke out in 1914 their son Randall and daughter Dorothy continued to support the parish. Thus, for those who so prefer, the story of Neasden presented here can be read almost as a family saga spanning more than two centuries and touching the contemporary world in contexts as varied as farming and manufacturing, the law and the Army.

But the main purpose of this book is to describe how the hamlet of Neasden changed as it was slowly transformed into a built-up suburb. There was still a substantial element of feudalism remaining when Willesden donned black for Joseph Nicoll's funeral in 1853 and when the whole parish went 'en fête' on a November day twenty years later for the wedding of Catherine Prout to a wealthy Scots landowner in St Mary's church. Already, however, wedding processions going down Neasden lane to Church End had to pass under a railway bridge and this symbolised the shape of things to come at Neasden. Over the next hundred years the hamlet was to be altered, piece by piece, to meet the needs of modern transport stemming firstly from the railways and afterwards from the roads, but always mainly in the interests of 'through' traffic.

Relations between Neasden and the railways were naturally influenced by its geographical position at the western end of the Dollis Hill ridge; and the two estates of railway cottages at Neasden were both built in low ground at some distance from the old road junction at the top. Another kind of transport business also found Neasden attractive as the first open country on the north-west outskirts of London: demand for horses in London soared in the second half of the Victorian period and many of Neasden's farms at this time concentrated on the rearing and pasturage of horses — an activity which later declined rapidly when petrol-fuelled transport got into its stride.

Always in the background was the slow outward spread of population from the metropolis which led to the final transformation of Neasden. During Queen Victoria's reign the population of England doubled, almost all of the increase taking place in the towns, where steam-powered factories ran on coal brought in by the railways. London spread into Willesden in the form of a ring joining Kensal Green, Harlesden, Church End, Willesden Green and Kilburn. It was not until Edwardian times that the housing tide reached the London end of Neasden, causing the new St Catherine's church to be built not near the Metropolitan railway estate, as originally intended, but at the old centre of Neasden at the junction of the roads.

Local history, however, is not solely or even mainly about buildings; it should also tell about people, their thoughts and aspirations. In Willesden a great struggle went on during the last half of Queen Victoria's reign between the agricultural north, whose farmers had in the past dominated the Vestry, and the urbanised south which wanted more say in local affairs. The south won the most important battle in this Thirty Years War when it got the Willesden Local Board established with 50.2 per cent of the votes cast. The head-on clash of interests was made particularly violent by the presence of the Brondesbury ridge, effectively dividing Willesden into two drainage areas. The southerners, with their permanent 9/6 majority on the Board, imposed a separate system on the north in the 1880s based on Neasden sewage farm, but twenty years later all agreed that this had been a mistake. The antagonism and resentment took longer to disappear.

About a hundred years ago, landowners like Prout who represented the old tradition were disappearing from the scene while well-to-do people moved into Neasden's large houses from outside. In the 18th century it had been common for these to be used as country seats by people with houses and business in London, like the politician General Lord George Carpenter at the Grove and the surgeon Percivall Pott at Neasden House. Similarly in the last two decades of the Victorian period quite a number of west-end professional men came to Neasden, like the vets Rotherham and South and the art-dealer Beeforth. At this time too, Dollis Hill House was used by the Earl of Aberdeen as a country seat to which W.E. Gladstone and other Liberal politicians were frequently invited to refresh themselves in surroundings of rural tranquillity. Neasden House itself became the home of a golf club catering not for any local demand but for well-connected people from London's west end and the north-west suburbs; and several members from the West Hampstead area decided to settle in Neasden near the club, like the manufacturers Tubbs and Glanfield.

It is clear enough now that what decisively changed things at Neasden was the decision to build the North Circular Road through the centre of the place. Had this ring-road been built north of the Brent, where the abortive Outer Circle railway had been planned to run, the future of Neasden would without doubt have been very different. Neasden remained attractively rural until after the 1914–18 war and in the 1920s there was a vigorous community life in Neasden Village, as the railway cottage estate was normally known. This changed when from the late 1920s the old centre of Neasden at the old road junction reasserted itself.

As the builders moved into the golf course the golf club was disbanded while the front part of Neasden House was converted into flats before being finally demolished in 1938. The population of Neasden parish grew so fast that the northern boundary had to be pulled back about a mile. The Council built Neasden's public library in 1931 (in the wrong place) and the Ritz cinema from 1935 served for a generation as a useful cultural centre. But a sense of community, so lively in the old Neasden Village, never successfully developed in the new Neasden. The spirit of the old Neasden largely disappeared with the last of the green fields.

Developments since 1945 have only made things worse. Road traffic increased inexorably on both the North Circular ring-road and the Neasden Lane radial road, and when the underpass was constructed in an attempt to solve the intersection problem the cohesion of Neasden was destroyed. This was the bitter harvest of the decision taken sixty years previously to construct the ring-road right through the centre of Neasden. Harlesden and Wembley, each lying about a mile away from the road, were able to escape destruction; but Neasden got it in the neck. It will not be easy to revitalise a place whose cohesion and sense of identity have been so severely impaired; but a greater awareness of its historical past may help.

Neasden folk old enough to remember the green fields of fifty years ago invariably speak wistfully of the pretty place it used to be; they will read this book with a sense of personal loss. But such people are a dwindling minority. The many who have no knowledge of the old Neasden nevertheless ask what it was like when it was fields. The story which follows may help to answer this question. At the end of the book we take four walks about present-day Neasden to look at what remains from former times and to try to relate the present to the past. For some this will revive memories; for most it will require a considerable effort of imagination as so much is now so different. For everyone the walks should in some sense be rewarding.

Spelling

Over the centuries the name Neasden, like most place-names, has been spelt in a great many ways, e.g. Neosdune, Nesedon, Nesdon, Nesden, Neesden, Neasdon. In early times, when formal documents were written in Latin, the suffix 'don' (= hill) seems to have been universal. Michael Roberts in the 16th century wrote 'Neasdon' and this was the normal spelling from early in the 18th century until the arrival of the Metropolitan railway finally standardised it as 'Neasden'. But in the 17th century 'Neesden' was more common. In this study the spelling of Neasden most common in each historical period has been used.

Similarly what is now 'Dollis Hill' was normally 'Dolley's hill' in the 18th century while 'Dudden Hill' has always been 'Dudding hill' to the railways. In such cases the spelling most appropriate to the context has been used. The modern practice of using capital letters for words like Road, Hill, etc has been followed only for the post-1945 period.

PART ONE
Before 1800

THE HISTORY OF WILLESDEN has been influenced in an important way by two ridges of high ground which run across it. The Brondesbury ridge extends by way of Shoot-up hill from the heights of Hampstead to Harlesden, forming an east-west watershed across the old parish. About a mile to the north of it, the shorter Dollis-hill ridge rises abruptly from the Edgware road in the east and narrows to a point at its western end about a mile away. On the broader eastern end stood Oxgate, on the summit in the centre stood Dollis Hill and at its lower western end, on a sort of promontory, was the hamlet of Neasden.

The name Neasden has been spelt from time to time, as might be expected, in a variety of ways but the earliest spellings (e.g.Neosdune) suggest that it is connected with 'nose' (French equivalent 'nez'). The hamlet was regarded as consisting not only of the farms and houses at the west end of the Dollis (often Dolley's) hill ridge but also of the slopes leading down to the low ground on all sides but the east. About a kilometre away to the north the little river Brent flowed first west, then south, towards Brentford; and the marshy tract of land near the river downstream from Kingsbury bridge was known as Neasdon Bottom. The southern slopes of the ridge were steeper; so the Slade brook ('slade' = 'valley'), running from Cricklewood through Sherrick green, was barely half a mile away. To the west, the Slade brook took a long time to join up with the Brent at Stonebridge on the London-to-Harrow road and along this stretch of low-lying land the extent of Neasden was imprecise. In parish records in the 18th century Norman's farm, which abutted on the Harrow road just south of Stonebridge, was included in 'Neasdon' but it had earlier been included under 'Church End' and the change could well have been made partly because it happened to be owned by the Nicoll family of Neasdon, so that it was convenient to group it with their other holdings for such purposes as parish rates and land tax.

From Neasdon Top, as we may describe the nose of the promontory where several roads converged, there were extensive views across the valleys to Kingsbury in the north, to Harrow in the west, to Harlesden in the south and across the isolated Duddinghill, on whose summit stood a windmill, to the long line of the Brondesbury ridge. On this natural vantage-point a succession of houses stood for centuries. Lysons tells us that John Attewode owned the site in the reign of Richard I, while a writer early in Queen Anne's reign says that another John Attewode sold the property in 1403 to the Roberts family.[1]

A: The Roberts Era

In Edward IV's reign John Roberts (d. 1476) was described as coroner of Middlesex and holder of land 'within the manor of Nesdon'. In the reign of Henry VIII Thomas Roberts, a lawyer who resided mainly near St Clement Danes where he was buried in 1543, built or enlarged the house at Neasdon known as 'Catwoods'.[2] His second son Edmund Roberts, who succeeded to the property some time after his elder brother Michael died in 1544, married Frances daughter of Richard Welles of Ware (a Chancery clerk) in 1549 at Royston, Herts. At this time Royston manor was held by Robert Chester under grant from Henry VIII, to whom he had been a gentleman-usher of the royal chamber. At the christening of Francis, the first child of the marriage, at Royston in 1551 Chester, who was knighted soon afterwards, was joint godfather with Sir Robert Tyrwhitt, lord lieutenant of Huntingdonshire and former Master of the Horse to his relation Queen Catherine Parr; and when a year later the next child was christened Catherine (after her grandmother Catherine Welles) in St Mary's Willesden, Lady Catherine Chester stood as her godmother. Clearly by this time the Roberts family were well-connected.

Francis Roberts (1551–1631) married Mary Barne, granddaughter of Sir George Barne (Lord Mayor of London in 1552); but his eldest son Barne Roberts (1576–1611) lived with his wife Anne (daughter of Alderman Sir William Glover) not at Neasdon but near St Stephen's Coleman-street in the City. There in April 1604 twin sons were born to them: Barne Roberts 'the younger', who died at Eton College in 1618, and William, named after his grandfather, who entered Gray's Inn in 1622 and married Eleanor Atye a few months before being knighted by James I at Greenwich in 1624.[3]

When the Civil War broke out Sir William Roberts was a staunch supporter of Oliver Cromwell. In January 1649 he was one of the 135 commissioners nominated by Parliament to try King Charles but like half of the nominees he wisely declined to serve. He sat in the Barebones Parliament of 1653 and in the Parliaments of 1654 and 1656 as one of the four members for Middlesex.* He was appointed a member of the Council of State in 1653 and was called in 1657 to sit in the House of Lords, where he attended regularly during the protectorates of both Oliver and Richard Cromwell. In addition he was one of the commissioners for the Excise from 1654 with an annual salary of £300 and an auditor of the Exchequer for another £500 a year. He died in September 1662, too soon for any reconciliation with Charles II to be possible.

However, the new king was not hostile to the Roberts family, and in November 1661 he conferred a baronetcy on Sir William's eldest surviving son William (b.1638) — an honour for which the recipient had to pay over £1,000.[4] Following the dissolution of the long Cavalier Parliament of 1661–79 Sir William was elected as one of the two members for Middlesex in the three short parliaments which sat between 1679 and 1681, after which Charles would have no more of their repeated attempts to exclude his Roman Catholic brother from succession to the throne and reigned for his last four years without a parliament.

The first baronet was succeeded in March 1688 by his son William (b.1659) on whose death without issue in 1698 the baronetcy expired. Ownership of Neesden then

**see Appendix I*

The ROBERTS Family Succession

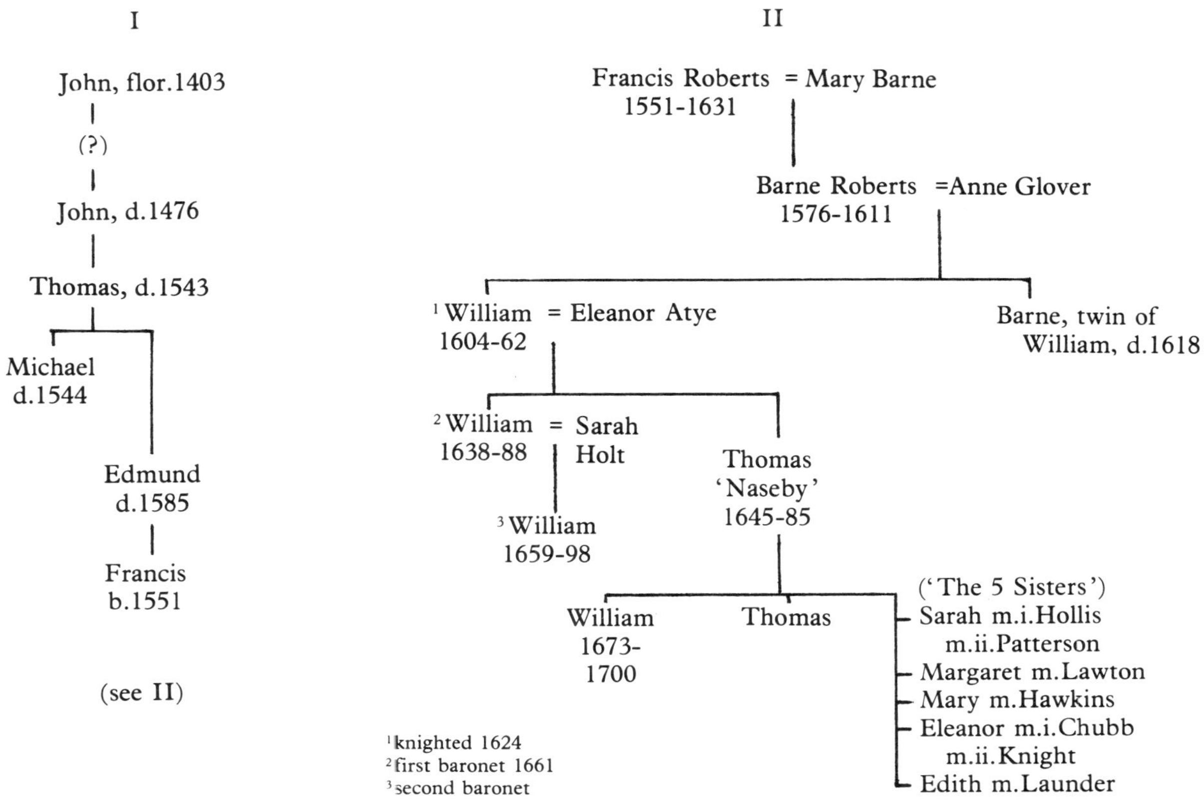

I

John, flor.1403
|
(?)
|
John, d.1476
|
Thomas, d.1543
- Michael d.1544
- Edmund d.1585
  - Francis b.1551

(see II)

II

Francis Roberts 1551-1631 = Mary Barne
- Barne Roberts 1576-1611 = Anne Glover
  - [1] William 1604-62 = Eleanor Atye
    - [2] William 1638-88 = Sarah Holt
      - [3] William 1659-98
    - Thomas 'Naseby' 1645-85
      - William 1673-1700
      - Thomas
      - ('The 5 Sisters')
        - Sarah m.i.Hollis m.ii.Patterson
        - Margaret m.Lawton
        - Mary m.Hawkins
        - Eleanor m.i.Chubb m.ii.Knight
        - Edith m.Launder
  - Barne, twin of William, d.1618

[1] knighted 1624
[2] first baronet 1661
[3] second baronet

passed to his younger cousin William (b.1673), son of the first baronet's brother Thomas 'Naseby' Roberts — who acquired his nickname because he was born soon after Fairfax's great victory in June 1645. This last William Roberts, who was neither knight nor baronet but simply esquire, died heirless in 1700 at the early age of 27.

As the 17th century came to a close the Roberts land empire was about to break up. Half a century earlier, the first Sir William Roberts had purchased in 1651 large areas of church lands which he and his forebears had previously held on lease, including the St Paul's cathedral prebends of Neesden, Oxgate and Harlesden and some land belonging to Westminster Abbey.* He appears to have greatly enlarged Neesden House in or about 1656 and to have enclosed the property with a brick wall, redrawing in the process the line of the lane (Bowre lane) which ran eastwards towards Dolley's hill in such a way as to enclose a piece of waste land, for which the family later had to pay a rent.[5] When he died in September 1662, leaving parts of the estate to his younger children, the young Sir William, displeased that as the eldest son he had not been left the whole estate, alleged that this part of the will was a forgery and not in his father's hand. In reply his mother Dame Eleanor (Elienor) assured the Lord Chancellor the Earl of Clarendon that the will was genuine, and probate was granted a few weeks later.

The last William Roberts sold off several large chunks of the family estates for nearly £4,000 in September 1700, three months before he died. His only son having died in infancy in the same year, he bequeathed Neesden in the first instance to his brother Thomas, who evidently died soon afterwards, and thereafter to his five sisters, after providing for his wife Elizabeth. This lady, a daughter of Lord Howard of Effingham (who was a descendant of Queen Elizabeth's admiral and himself governor of Virginia) did not long remain a widow before she married William Hutchenson, who was in 1706 head clerk in the Pells Office of the Exchequer and was later deputy chamberlain in the Receipt office. Elizabeth died in Kensington in 1728, Hutchenson in 1724.

In the meantime the Neesden lands had passed to the five sisters in 'one-fifth parts'. These one-fifth parts were later divided again among different purchasers so that there were in some cases 'a tenth part of a fifth part' or 'a quarter of a third of a fifth part'; this did not mean, however, that the estate was split up physically into fifty or sixty parts but simply that the income from the estate had to be so divided.

B: The First of the Nicolls

During the next century and a half a family called Nicoll gradually acquired most of these bits and pieces until they owned practically all the land in Neasdon. The name of Thomas Nicoll first occurs in the parish records of Willesden when he paid a poor-rate contribution of 10 shillings in 1719 on a farm valued at £80 a year which he occupied; this was Neasdon Farm, previously tenanted by Bartholomew Elliott, which was much the largest farm in the hamlet with an area at that time of about 130 acres.

By degrees Thomas Nicoll established himself at Neasdon. In particular, he quickly got involved in two charities which had been bestowed on Willesden by the Roberts family and were specifically linked to Neasdon House. The first of these charities had

*see *Appendix II*

an annual value of £2 and was founded by Francis Roberts, grandfather of the first Sir William, in 1624, the first payment to be made at the first Michaelmas after his death.[6] The system was that 'ten of the most substantial men of the parish' should act as trustees for collecting and paying over the £2 to the churchwardens for distribution among the poor of Willesden 'where most neede shall be'. Naturally the number of trustees would shrink over time but no action was to be taken until the number was down to four, when the survivors would nominate six more to join them.*

On 18th May 1660, a few days before Charles II landed at Dover to restore the monarchy, Sir William Roberts did Willesden a good turn. He noted that the ten trustees appointed by his grandfather were all deceased, rendering the gift 'voidable', but decided that notwithstanding the 'default and negligence' of the trustees he would reaffirm his grandfather's gift, while reserving to himself during his lifetime and thereafter to 'the owner of the capital messuage at Neesden' (i.e. Neesden House) both the nomination of the poor persons who were to benefit and the distribution of the money.[7] He also stated:

> 'There is in my hand the sum of one hundred and threescore pounds which I procured from the State for the releiving of the poor of the parish of Willesden with coale...'

Armed with this capital sum of £160 Sir William was able to grant in perpetuity an annual sum of £8 for expenditure on coal

> 'reserving to myself the nomination of the poor and the distribution of the said coales to them in proportion to their needs and necessities during my naturall life and after my decease to the owner of the capitall messuage at Neesden.'

Sir William also modified slightly his grandfather's system for replenishing the panel of trustees so that, when the number had shrunk to six (not four), the survivors should appoint four others.

A quarter of a century later it was alleged that Sir William had only reinstated his grandfather's gift, and started his own, in order to avoid being brought to book for trying to suppress the original charity.[8] However this may be, certainly his son (the first baronet) tried to conceal the charities after selling off the property from whose rent income they were nourished. A case was taken by the churchwardens of the parish, Robert Twyford and Edward Cockman, to the court of Chancery, which found in 1687 against the baronet; and in October 1688 his successor agreed that the annual sums for the charities would come from other lands still in his possession, including a Three Corner Field which would provide the £2 a year for the original charity.[9] Ten trustees were appointed, with provision for six others to be added when there were only four survivors (a reversion to Francis Roberts' original system).

In the Chancery court case Twyford had laid out over £30 in legal expenses, towards which the parish's poor-rate collections contributed £30 — evidence of the importance which the parish attached to the preservation of these charities. Proud of their success and needing at the same time to justify the appearance of such a large item of expenditure in the accounts, the parish officers exceptionally recorded full details of

**see Appendix III, a*

how the two charities were distributed in the spring of 1688.* The £8 charity was divided between twenty recipients, including nine widows, who received sums ranging from 5 to 15 shillings each in multiples of half-crowns. There were four recipients of the half-year distribution of the smaller £2 charity.

In 1722 when William Hutchenson and Thomas Wilkinson were the only surviving trustees, six more were added including Thomas Nicoll. After another forty-five years without further appointments old Thomas Nicoll, being then the sole survivor from the 1722 list as well as part-owner of Neasdon House, nominated a new list of ten trustees in 1767 including his sons Thomas and Joseph and his neighbours Francis Page of Dolley's hill and Edmund Franklyn of Oxgate.† As regards the income for the charities, there was no difficulty about the Three Corner Field, known as the Little Six Acres, because it was linked to Wilson's farm which adjoined Neasdon House and was occupied and partly owned by Thomas Nicoll. But the owner of the property from which the larger charity was nourished refused after 1766 to pay the £8 a year. So the churchwardens Thomas Nicoll the younger and his relation John Haley of Kilburn got the Attorney General to bring a case in the court of Chancery in 1769 which had a successful outcome two years later.

Besides looking after the charities Thomas Nicoll the elder did more than his fair share of filling the various unpaid offices such as churchwarden and overseer of the poor, to which appointments were made annually by the parishioners voting at the parish Vestry. Thomas had his first spell as churchwarden in 1724 and as overseer in 1728 and over the next thirty years his name is to be found as often as not in one or other of the parish offices each year. In 1755 a list of alterations to the Commission of the Peace for Middlesex shows 'Thomas Niccoll of Willsden, Esq' among the additions and it was confirmed in the following year that he had the necessary property qualification of £100 a year to act as a Justice and had been assigned to keep the peace in the County and 'to hear and determine divers Felonies, Trespasses and other Misdeeds committed in the same County'. One of the most important functions of a Justice was to keep an eye on the way the parish officers did their jobs; and Thomas Nicoll was one of the two Justices who approved the Willesden poor-rate lists in 1770, 1771 and 1772 when the poundages were 4d, 6d and 4d in the £ respectively.

Over the years Thomas Nicoll gradually expanded his holdings of land at Neasdon. By 1730 he was working not only Neasdon Farm but also about 60 acres known as 'the hospital land'.[10] This was the local phrase for the land acquired from the legatees of the Roberts family in 1704 by Christ's Hospital (the bluecoat school) acting on behalf of the parish of Wandsworth. The will of Francis Millington, who was both a resident of Wandsworth and a governor of Christ's hospital, had given the hospital governors in 1693 the job of purchasing £500 worth of land within one hundred miles of London from which the annual income would be passed to the vicar and churchwardens of Wandsworth to be used for the relief and maintenance of 'poor seamen and watermen of 50 years and upwards born and dwelling in the town or parish of Wandsworth' who had been disabled somehow at sea or on the water. The Wandsworth authorities were to draw up the initial list of beneficiaries and adjust it subsequently, year by year, as

*see *Appendix III, b*

†see *Appendix III, a*

Neasdon's Farms in the 18th century

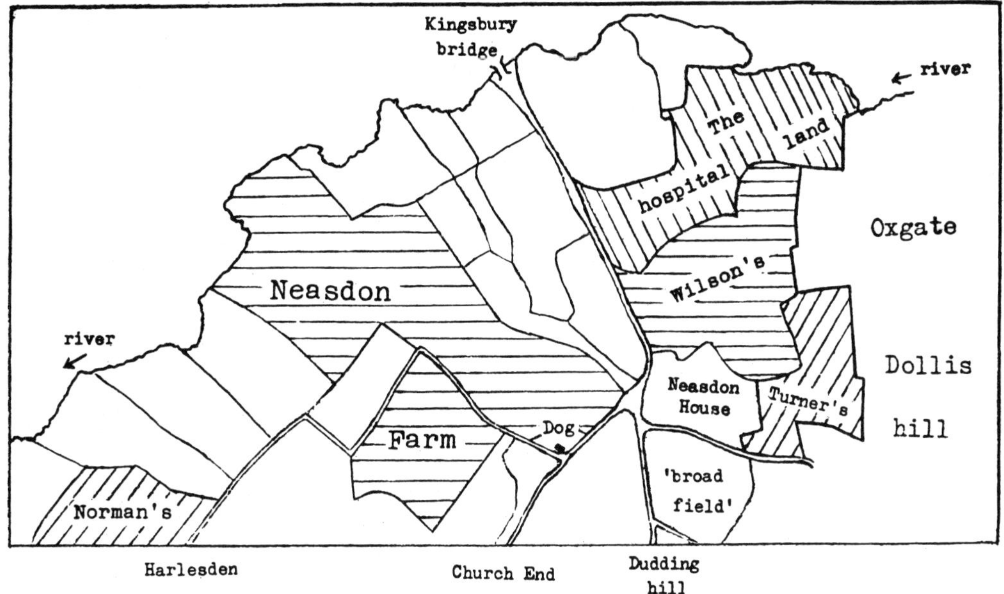

necessary. Some of the money was to be distributed in cash and some in the form of bluecloth almscoats to be given out at Michaelmas before the onset of winter.

The 'Wilsdon lands' purchased by Christ's Hospital in 1704 lay mainly east of the road leading down from Neasdon Top to Kingsbury bridge and abutted on the river. Half of the purchase cost of £1,080 for the 60-odd acres came from the Millington charity account, the £540 being made up of the £500 bequest plus a further £40 donated to the charity by a trustee John Emilie. The other half came from two other Wandsworth charities: £360 from Sir Allen Broderick's charity and £180 from Nicholas Tonnet's.

The estate was managed wholly by the hospital governors who selected the tenants and fixed and collected the rents. The first tenants were Charles Hunt and his wife, who stayed on as tenant after being widowed. In about 1730 Thomas Nicoll obtained the tenancy, which was to remain with the family for over forty years.

Soon after the middle of the century Thomas took on three more medium-sized farms, bringing his rateable value to well over half of the total for Neasdon. Wilson's Farm, named after a local landowner John Wilson who had occupied it himself for many years, adjoined the parkland of Neasdon House on the north and east sides; and Thomas Nicoll took over the house and the farm in or soon after 1752. Another holding was that of Turner's Farm which was occupied for a few years in the 1740s by the small farmer James Turner; this farm adjoined the south side of Wilson's and for a short distance fronted the lane to Dolley's hill. The third was Norman's Farm, which lay

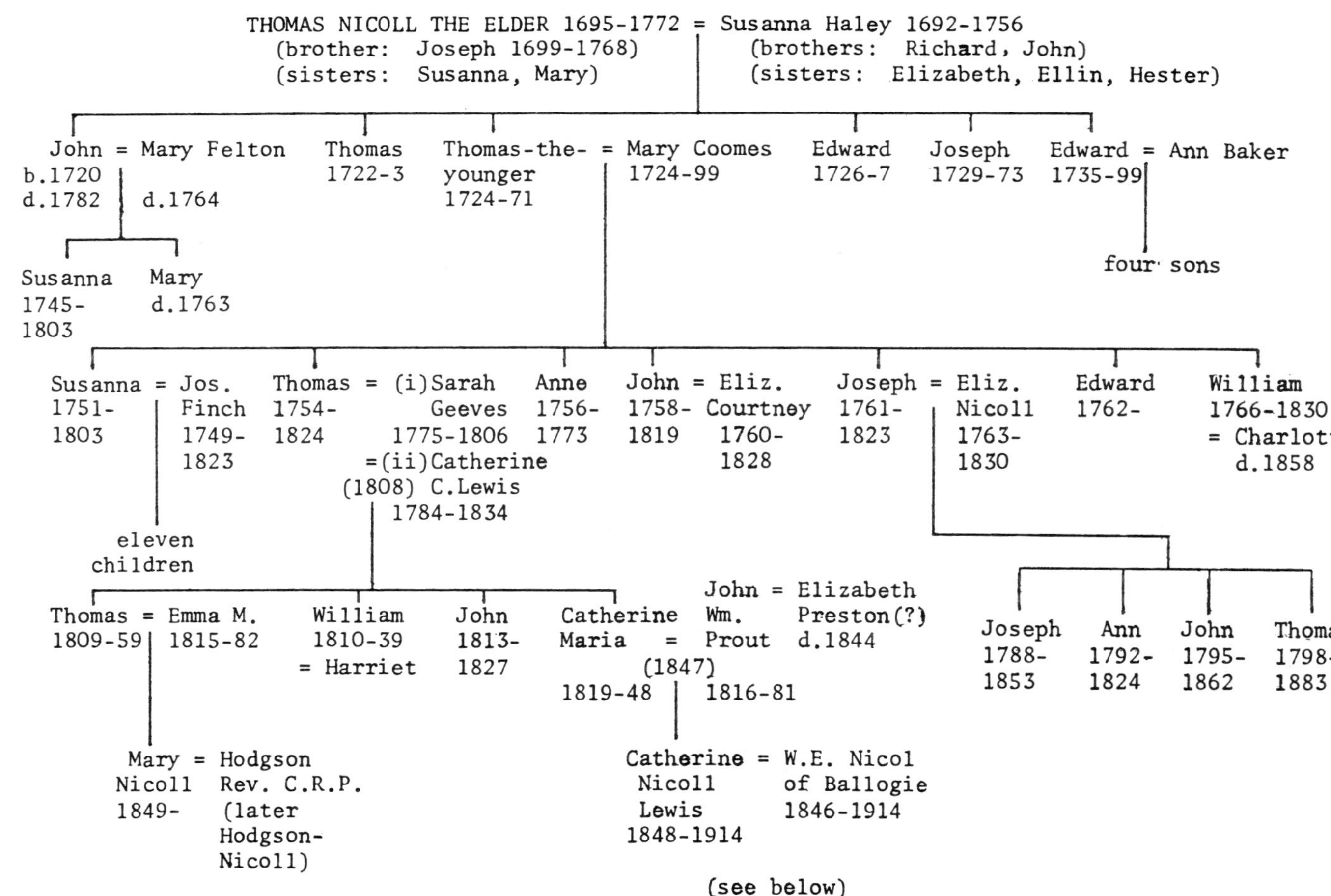
The NICOLL family of NEASDON
THOMAS NICOLL THE ELDER 1695-1772 = Susanna Haley 1692-1756
(brother: Joseph 1699-1768)
(sisters: Susanna, Mary)
(brothers: Richard, John)
(sisters: Elizabeth, Ellin, Hester)
John = Mary Felton
b.1720
d.1782
d.1764
Susanna 1745-1803
Mary d.1763
Thomas 1722-3
Thomas-the-younger 1724-71 = Mary Coomes 1724-99
Edward 1726-7
Joseph 1729-73
Edward 1735-99 = Ann Baker
four sons
Susanna 1751-1803 = Jos. Finch 1749-1823
eleven children
Thomas 1754-1824 = (i)Sarah Geeves 1775-1806
=(ii)Catherine (1808) C.Lewis 1784-1834
Anne 1756-1773
John 1758-1819 = Eliz. Courtney 1760-1828
Joseph 1761-1823 = Eliz. Nicoll 1763-1830
Edward 1762-
William 1766-1830 = Charlotte d.1858
Joseph 1788-1853
Ann 1792-1824
John 1795-1862
Thomas 1798-1883
Thomas 1809-59 = Emma M. 1815-82
William 1810-39 = Harriet
John 1813-1827
Catherine Maria 1819-48 = (1847) John Wm. Prout 1816-81
John = Elizabeth Preston(?) d.1844
Mary Nicoll 1849- = Hodgson Rev. C.R.P. (later Hodgson-Nicoll)
Catherine Nicoll Lewis 1848-1914 = W.E. Nicol of Ballogie 1846-1914
(see below)

The PROUTs and the NICOLs

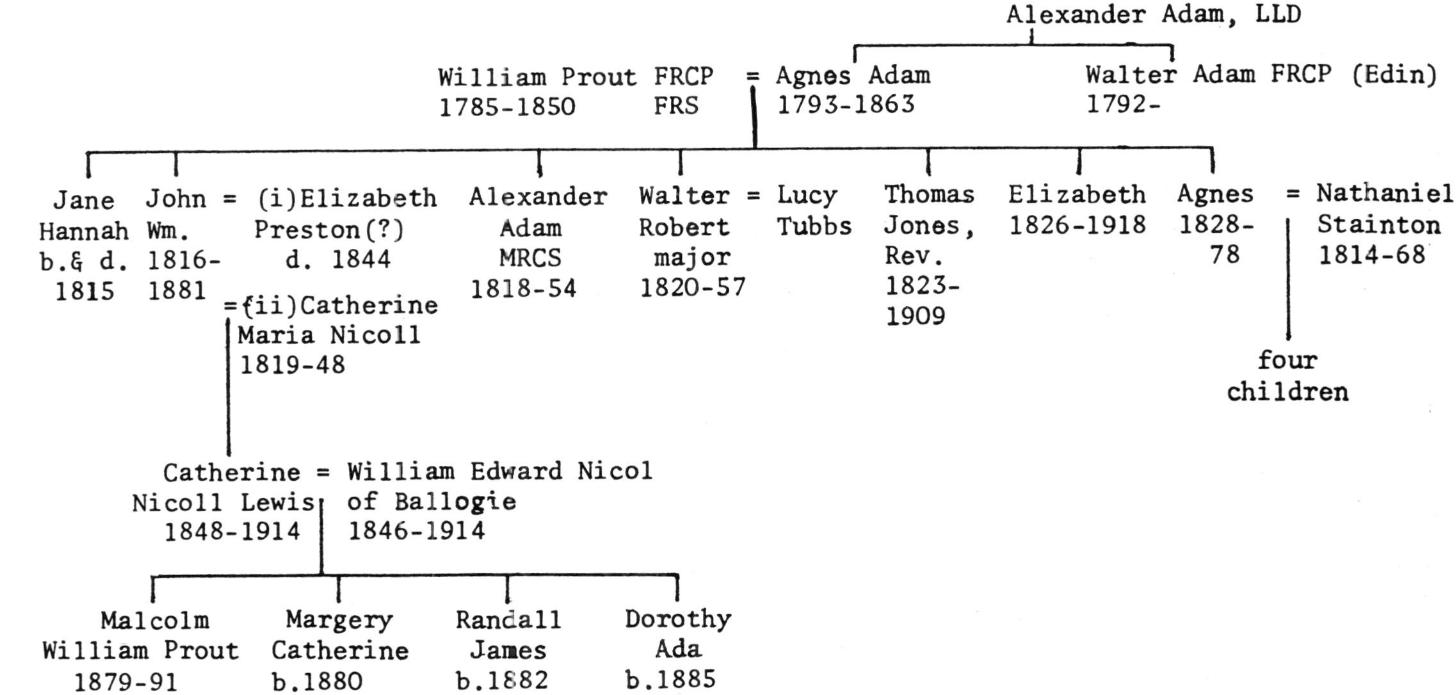

about a mile from Neasdon Top in the low ground running towards the stone bridge on the London-to-Harrow road; it had previously belonged to the Sibleys of Studham, who were related to Thomas Nicoll.

But although by 1755 Thomas Nicoll had become by far the most prominent of Neasdon's inhabitants his land ownership was still quite modest. Neither he nor his sons had any share in the ownership of Neasdon Farm or of the hospital land, and he had only a minority share in Neasdon House and Wilson's Farm. The largest landowner in Neasdon was in fact the Marquis of Carnarvon who had acquired much of it as a result of marrying an heiress of a branch of the Nicoll family living in the area of Southgate and Colney Hatch. John Nicoll senior of Southgate (d. 1731) was appointed county sheriff in 1720 but bought himself out of the job (being 'fined for sheriff'); later he was a director of the Bank of England. Both John senior and John junior his son (d. 1747) chose, as wealthy people often did, to be buried in linen (in Friern Barnet churchyard), the family paying the statutory penalty for not burying them in woollen clothes.[11] John junior was evidently a lawyer and is variously described as being of Queen's Square Bloomsbury, of Lincoln's Inn and of Southgate, where he owned Minchenden House. He also acquired quite a lot of the former Roberts land at Neasdon, some of it from John Wilson in the form of one or more of the 'fifth-parts', which on his death passed in trust to his only child Margaret, then a minor aged thirteen. In 1752 a marriage was arranged, on terms approved by the court of Chancery, between Margaret Nicoll and James Brydges, Marquis of Carnarvon and heir apparent of the Duke of Chandos. When the marriage took place in 1753 Margaret's lands passed into the Brydges empire, though they were kept separate in the accounts.[12] The marchioness died childless in 1768, three years before James succeeded to the dukedom, and was given a splendid monument in the church of St Lawrence Whitchurch near Edgware.

So when Thomas died at Neasdon in 1772 much of the hamlet belonged to the Duke of Chandos, including a three-fifths interest in Neasdon House; and Thomas refers specifically in his will to the 'two undivided fifth parts' of the property which were his. In some other lands the Duke had a half-interest (for instance a 'moiety' of Turner's Farm, Thomas having the other half) or a four-fifths interest (as in land on Dolley's hill where Thomas had the other fifth) or the whole of the estate (as in the case of Neasdon Farm). In practice, however, the Duke's land was occupied by the Nicolls and others on leases of various kinds.

Thomas Nicoll's origins are not easy to establish. Family records show that his parents were Edward Nicoll and Mary (*née* Pedder) and the Totteridge parish registers record the christening of a son Thomas belonging to such parents in July 1695, a daughter Susanna in 1691 and a boy John in 1694 who died in infancy. Thomas's younger brother Joseph seems to be recorded in the Hendon St Mary's register in 1699 where Edward the father is described as a farmer. Joseph was later associated with Thomas in land transactions over a long period and was referred to in a deed dated 1726 as being of Twyford, where he was a tenant farmer for eight or nine years before moving permanently to the Barnet area to farm about 150 acres. Joseph died at Barnet in 1768 but was buried in Totteridge churchyard. Having no surviving children to succeed him, Joseph left his property in the first instance to his wife, who died in the following year, and thereafter to his nephews the sons of Thomas. Of a younger sister Mary little is known except that she lived for many years as widow Harris in a house on Highwood hill, dying in 1762.

In 1718 or 1719 Thomas Nicoll married Susanna, daughter of Richard Haley of Mill Hill, who had been christened at Hendon in 1692. Susan, as she was called within the family, had three sisters including Elizabeth who married George Marsh, joint occupier with his brother of the Ewe inn. The Haleys had other alehouse connexions. Henry Haley had an inn at Gutter's Hedge in the south of Hendon overlooking the river Brent, and later John Haley, Susan's younger brother, had the King's Head at Mill Hill and the Crane at Edgware. Her elder brother Richard, who farmed on Dolley's hill next door to Neasdon for about twenty years from 1730, was frequently one of the Willesden parish churchwardens.

The Nicoll family had many branches in and north of Hendon from Edgware across to Southgate, and in Hertfordshire. How the Nicoll family grew at Neasdon from 1720 onwards is illustrated by the genealogical tree. Thomas Nicoll the elder always signed himself 'Niccoll', as did his brother Joseph, but it seems to have been agreed within the family that 'Nicoll' should be used for succeeding generations, possibly in order to harmonise the spelling with that used by the branches of the family in and around Hendon.

The first child born to Thomas and Susanna was christened John in St Mary's Willesden in 1720, with John Nicoll of Hendon standing as godfather. In February 1740, at the age of 19, John was admitted to membership of the Middle Temple in London as

> 'John Niccoll, son and heir of Thomas Niccoll of Neasdon in the Parish of Willesden, gent.'

Later he established a law business in Hatton Garden, Holborn, where John Nicoll of Southgate had had property, and he never subsequently lived in Neasdon. In 1753 his godfather died at Copt Hall in Page-street, about a mile north of Hendon church, leaving the bulk of his estate in the first instance to his brother-in-law James Ingram of Barnet (a Doctor of Physick) and thereafter to his godson John. So when Ingram died in 1755 John Nicoll came into the ownership of Copt Hall and other estates in and north of Hendon.

Thomas's second child, born in 1722, was named after his father but died at the age of ten months and was buried in Hendon churchyard. Another Thomas was born in 1724 and became known later as Thomas Nicoll the younger and as his father's 'second' son. Young Thomas had the soul of a farmer. As a young man he had the tenure of Notting Barns farm in north Kensington and attended regularly for some years about 1750 at the Kensington parish Vestry. It is recorded in one year that farmer Nicoll was paid a shilling by the churchwardens for catching a polecat. He was already married to Mary daughter of William Coomes of the Hyde, Hendon, whose dowry of £400 was subject to five years' deferment, during which time interest was paid quarterly to Thomas at the annual rate of £15. About the time that the capital became payable in 1753 Thomas Nicoll the elder moved into Neasdon House, taking on

Wilson's and Turner's farms, while the younger Thomas returned from Kensington to become tenant of Neasdon Farm and of the hospital land hitherto occupied by his father; and in later years he gradually took over other lands from his father.

The younger Thomas was no more averse than his father to shouldering the burdens of parish office. He was churchwarden continuously in the decade preceding his death in 1771 and it was on his initiative that the court of Chancery was asked to protect the larger of the Neasdon House charities. In 1769 he was added to the list of Justices for Middlesex and a document survives which records the sovereign's 'dedimus potestatem' authorising the royal Chancery to accept the oaths of

> 'our beloved and faithful John Wright, Percival Hart and Thomas Nicol the Younger Esquires Keepers of our Peace in the county of Middlesex' (GLRO: MJP/0/1)

When he died eighteen months before his father in March 1771 Thomas left a widow and seven children of whom the eldest was Susanna, born in 1751 when her parents were living in Kensington. He left his pieces of land, including the vast 18-acre field called 'broadfield' which lay between Dolley's hill lane, Dudding hill lane and the Slade brook, partly to his eldest son Thomas (b. 1754), partly to John (b. 1758) and partly to Joseph (b. 1761). He left legacies of money to Susanna, Ann (b. 1756), Edward (b. 1762) and William (b. 1766); he also remembered his niece Susanna, daughter of his brother John of Page-street. But his chief concern was to provide for the continuation of his 'farming business' which covered in all some three hundred acres.

Included in Thomas's bequests to his brother Joseph was property 'at a certain place called Wilsdon Green in the parish of Wilsdon known by the Name or Sign of the Dogg'. Thomas had acquired this property, which seems to have been licensed as The Dogg at least as early as 1729, through his brother Edward in 1767, and in the same year the name of Spotted Dog was given to the licensed house owned by the Nicolls at Neasdon.* In 1722 Richard Goldington had a licence at Neasdon Great House, of which he was then the occupier, but records for this period are scanty. However, the Kensington licensing lists show that premises called 'The Angel' at Neasdon had a licence going back at least to 1751 and in one year (1763) Thomas Nicoll himself was the licensee. The Angel stayed in the lists until 1767 but was thereafter replaced by The Dog or Spotted Dog. It seems probable that this Spotted Dog was the former 'Angel' under a new name and should be identified with the building shown on Rocque's map of 1746 at the corner of the lane later called Dog lane but then known as Stones lane, no doubt because it led down to fields called Great, Middle and Little Stones, which were part of Neasdon Farm near the river.

Thomas Nicoll the elder's fourth child, born in 1726 and christened with the name of Edward, died at the age of 15 months but the name Edward was not used for the next child, born in 1729, who was called Joseph. Joseph became an apprentice at the Royal Mint in the Tower of London in about 1745 and was always known as Thomas's 'third' son. The list of Thomas's children is completed by another Edward, born in 1735, who lived for a time at the Hyde, Hendon, and owned the 'Spotted Dog' at Willesden Green, as we have seen, for a short period.

**see Appendix IV*

Thomas therefore had three surviving sons to consider when making his will in 1772. Susan his wife had been buried in 1756 in a new vault for the Neasdon Nicolls in Hendon churchyard adorned with the Nicoll and Haley arms and purchased from the parish at the usual price of 8 guineas. The natural successor to Thomas's property would therefore have been his eldest son John. But although John, like his unmarried daughter Susanna, got a small bequest of £100 he was deliberately cut out of his father's property because he already had 'a very ample estate and fortune of his own'. Although the meaning of this phrase was not spelt out it undoubtedly referred to John's valuable inheritance at Copt hall, Hendon. In broad terms Thomas left Neasdon to his third son Joseph and his Hertfordshire lands to his fourth son Edward; he made separate provision for his five grandsons (the sons of Thomas the younger), their mother Mary and her two daughters.

In August 1772 Thomas Nicoll the elder joined his wife in the vault in Hendon churchyard after spending over half a century at Neasdon putting down roots for his family. His services to Willesden parish over this time seem to have been exemplary and he attracted none of the criticism of the sort directed previously against the Roberts family and later against his great-grandson Joseph. His death, noted in the *Gentleman's Magazine*, marks the end of a chapter in the story of Neasdon.

C: A Quiet Interlude

Thomas-the-elder had lain only six months in Hendon churchyard when he was joined there by his son and successor Joseph. By profession Joseph was a fellow of the Company of Moneyers at the Royal Mint, into which he was probably introduced in 1745 or thereabouts by his uncle John Haley of Mill Hill; and in 1773 his own nephew John (b. 1758) was marked out for an apprenticeship in the same line of business. The unmarried Joseph, who desired in his will to be buried in the Hendon vault 'as near the remains of my dear mother as conveniently may be', left his Neasdon property in the first instance to his well-to-do elder brother John of Page-street but on condition that it should pass later to his nephew John (b. 1758) who was to succeed him at the Mint. Evidently Joseph had a liking for the pictorial arts since he refers in his will to 'all my pictures and prints of every sort'. He also took care to protect his unmarried niece Susanna (b. 1745) by giving her an option to live at Neasdon House for one year after her father's death if she so wished; and the Sibleys of Studham and John Haley of Kilburn were among those who got token bequests.

From 1773 therefore until his death in 1782 John Nicoll the lawyer (b. 1720) was the owner both of Copt hall, Hendon, and of the Nicoll interest in Neasdon House, as well as other property, but after his boyhood he seems never subsequently to have resided in Neasdon. He lived for a considerable time after 1755 at Hendon and then for a spell in the 1770s at Ashlyns in the parish of Berkhamsted St Peter, where he owned a farm and other property. But he faithfully carried out his responsibilites after 1773 as the titular head of Neasdon House and we find him in 1776 authorising a list of names submitted to him as the proposed beneficiaries of the Neasdon House charities in that year. At the foot of the list John made the comment

> 'I have no objection to the above list if the churchwardens and overseers of the poor approve thereof'

and he signed it 'John Nicoll, Neasdon House, 5th February 1776'. The parish authorities then added, opposite each name in the list, the amount which each of the beneficiaries should receive. In practice, therefore, the parish had a bigger say in the distribution of the charity money than Sir William Roberts had envisaged in 1660 when he reserved to Neasdon House the selection both of the beneficiaries and of the amounts to go to each.

Some time in the late 1770s John returned from Ashlyns to Copt Hall, Hendon, and when he died in 1782 he was buried not in his father's vault for the Neasdon Nicolls, but in the old vault for the Copt hall branch of the family close to the east wall of the church. The inscription for him on the vault, unlike the others, is in abbreviated Latin and tells us that he was 'Med Tem Lond Armig RSS' which should mean that he was a member of the Middle Temple in London, an Esquire and a Fellow of the Royal Society (regiae societatis sodalis). Certainly he belonged to the Middle Temple; and the Royal Society's records preserve a signature by a John Nicoll, elected Fellow in 1765, which is clearly from the same hand as the one in the Willesden records.

The wording of John's last will suggests that he had made earlier wills in considerable detail (perhaps as detailed as his daughter's will later which ran to ten large pages) but the will he wrote in January 1782 covered only one sheet of paper and left everything quite simply to Susanna. Susanna lived on unmarried at Copt hall until 1803 and a local farmer William Geeves farmed as tenant on the estate. She did not inherit the Nicoll interest in Neasdon because that had to pass, as directed by Joseph Nicoll (d. 1773), to John Nicoll (b. 1758) who entered the Royal Mint in January 1774.

It seems that Joseph had preferred to live near his work at the Mint rather than at Neasdon; and the new master of Neasdon House did the same. By 1782 young John had completed his seven-year apprenticeship and was a fully-fledged moneyer. In and soon after 1800 he is described as being 'of Tanfield Court in the Inner Temple', but this does not imply that he was a professional lawyer: members of the Temple could and did sublet their rooms freely to non-members and John probably had a subletting of this kind. Given the difficulties of commuting in those days, what with the mud and floods of winter, the summer dust, the permanent ruts dug deep into the roads and the constant threat of robbery by the highwaymen who infested the main roads out of London, including the turnpike road to Edgware, it is not surprising if people with daily business in London preferred to live during the week in rooms in the city, near to their work.

In the last quarter of the 18th century, when the Nicolls did not reside there, Neasdon House had a succession of tenants, of whom the most illustrious was Mr Percivall Pott. Not long after he was born in 1713 Percivall lost his father but was befriended by the bishop of Rochester, a distant relative of his mother's. He was apprenticed to a surgeon at St Bartholemew's hospital, became assistant surgeon in 1744 and later rose to be the hospital's principal surgeon and his profession's leading practitioner, teacher and writer. More than half a dozen medical conditions still bear his name, including 'Pott's fracture' which refers to a condition he himself sustained after being thrown from his horse in 1756. It was during convalescence after this accident that he took to writing surgical books. He was elected fellow of the Royal Society in 1764.

In 1784 Pott became the occupier of Neasdon House, though he retained his town house in Hanover-square at the corner of Princes-street and probably resided at Neasdon only for limited periods each year. In the autumn of his life he was elected the first-ever honorary fellow of Edinburgh's Royal College of Surgeons and also an honorary member of the analogous Irish college. When he retired from his surgical post at St Bartholomew's in 1787 he was appointed a governor of the hospital and received the green staff of office. Still practising privately, he died in London in December 1788 a few days after visiting patients in the country in bitter weather. His son-in-law Sir James Earle who later edited his surgical writings tells us in an introductory biographical note that almost his last words were 'My lamp is almost extinguished; I hope it has burned for the benefit of others'. He was able to make ample provision for his widow Sarah, who retained the occupancy of Neasdon House for a further three years, and for his four sons and four daughters. His second son Joseph, who was later to hold canonries at St Paul's and Exeter cathedrals, composed the long inscription for the memorial tablet erected in St Mary Aldermary; and in 1821, while archdeacon of St Albans, he preached the annual charity sermon in St Mary's Willesden in aid of the Willesden charities.

Among other tenants of Neasdon House in the last quarter of the century were Christopher Fowler, John Jackson, Thomas Croft and Alexander Bruce. Across the road, the house later called the Grove had been occupied by tenants for most of the second half of the century. The land was purchased by the Wingfields from William Roberts in September 1700 and the house was erected some time in the next few years, certainly by 1708. The Wingfields later moved away to Berkhamsted St Peter and Edward Carr became tenant until succeeded by Lord Carpenter. Carpenter, who was a lieutenant-general when he helped to put down the 1715 Jacobite rising, was a personal friend of General Wade, famous for the great military roads he built in Scotland, and of the Duke of Chandos, who helped Carpenter in his political career and described him once as 'a gentleman much in favour with the Court'. Besides being appointed governor of Minorca, Carpenter was M.P. for Whitchurch (Hants) with strong Whig sympathies in the 1715–22 Parliament and was one of the first residents in the new Hanover square in Westminster in 1720. In 1722 he became a member for the Westminster constituency after the two members originally elected had both been disqualified and it was during this 1722–27 Parliament that he acquired the Grove at Neasdon as a country house.* George's father's end had been hastened by wounds sustained in the royalist cause at Naseby (1645) where a musket ball went through both his legs; and George himself had all the teeth on one side of his mouth knocked out and his jaw broken by a musket ball during his service in Spain in Queen Anne's reign. His biographer Crull says that after being made a baron in 1719 a fall loosened all the rest of his teeth, so that he suffered severe eating difficulties until his death in 1732 on his 75th birthday. During his last few years he was churchwarden of the parish of St George's, Hanover square.

**see Appendix I*

A less eminent soldier, Captain Charles Rambouillet, acquired the Grove in 1734 and several of his children who died young lie buried in Willesden churchyard, where Rambouillet himself was interred in 1747. Among later tenants of the Rambouillet family was Samuel Spindler, who had a gold-refining business in Gutter lane, off Cheapside, and had been apprenticed in the Goldsmiths Company (one of the twelve great livery companies of London) in 1727.[13] He regularly attended the Trial of the Pyx, at which gold and silver coins recently produced at the Mint were periodically subjected to expert examination by command of the Lord Chancellor, and in 1764 he was prime warden (master) of the company. From 1760 he occupied the Grove at Neasdon, probably using it as a country seat as Pott later used Neasdon House. After his death in 1768 his widow Mary stayed on for several years, like Sarah Pott, before moving in 1773 to Windsor where she died in 1783. Though Samuel is not mentioned as attending the Willesden vestry, the Spindlers were evidently friendly with the Rev Moses Wight, vicar of St Mary's from 1764 to 1795, who was a minor canon in St Paul's cathedral (where he lies buried in the crypt) and minister of the Bridewell hospital. Samuel had a brother the Rev Bond Spindler, vicar of a Berkshire parish, and this may have had something to do with the fact that clergymen occupied the Grove for the next thirty years: first the Rev Raikes, then the Rev Bristow.

Richard Raikes, born in Gloucester in 1743, was the fourth son of the printer who founded the *Gloucester Journal* and the younger brother of Robert Raikes, the founder of many Sunday schools. After Eton he was a prizeman and medallist at Cambridge and fellow of St John's college from 1767 to 1775. Although ordained in 1772 it was only in 1793 that he received his first incumbency at Maisemore just outside Gloucester. He held this living until his death in 1823, becoming also treasurer (later canon) of St David's cathedral in Wales in 1797 and prebendary of Hereford in 1809. Richard suffered from poor health but he was held in great affection by the people of Gloucester, who contrasted his kindliness with the vanity displayed by his famous brother Robert. He was given a memorial tablet in Gloucester cathedral.

Raikes spent almost the whole time between 1772 and 1793 as a resident of Neasdon where he ran a residential preparatory school for the young sons of gentlemen of rank. He was already living in Neasdon when he married Anne Mee, a cousin of Lord Palmerston's mother, at the end of 1774. Ann naturally had a key role at the school which existed certainly throughout the 1780s and possibly for the whole time Raikes lived at Neasdon, dutifully paying his rates but apparently taking no active part in local affairs.

The brightest star of Raikes's Neasdon academy was probably George Howard (1773–1848) who bore from birth the title of Lord Morpeth. While his father, the Earl of Carlisle, was abroad in Ireland from 1780 to 1782 as lord-lieutenant, young George was under the fatherly eye of George Augustus Selwyn, politician and wit, who was a close friend of the Earl (both were old-Etonians). Selwyn's family seat was Matson House near Gloucester city, which he represented in Parliament from 1754 to 1780, and it was no doubt through Selwyn that Carlisle's son and heir came to Neasdon. Selwyn frequently visited George at Neasdon, sometimes in the company of the boy's maternal grandfather Lord Gower (later Marquis of Stafford), and he wrote many letters to the Earl giving him news about his son's progress and welfare at the school.

In these early days George already showed considerable literary ability which he developed further at Eton (1785–90) and Christ Church Oxford. In 1797–8, as 'Classical Correspondent', he contributed a number of verse compositions, modelled to some extent on the Latin odes of Horace, to the weekly paper *The Anti-Jacobin.* He was made F.R.S. in 1795, a Privy Counsellor in 1806 and, after succeeding to his father's title as sixth Earl of Carlisle in 1825, twice held office as Lord Privy Seal, receiving the Garter in 1837.

George's younger brother William, born in Ireland and nicknamed 'Paddy', was also educated at the school before going on to Eton but the Earl's third son Frederick, later killed at Waterloo and commemorated in Lord Byron's *Childe Harold,* was too young to be taught by Raikes. The most notable of the pupils apart from George Howard was probably Robert Eden who, after Eton and Cambridge, succeeded his father Sir John Eden as fifth baronet; he may have joined the school because his uncle William Eden (M.P. for Durham county, later Lord Auckland) was Carlisle's friend and colleague. It is not known whether the school continued under the Rev. John Bristow, who occupied the property after Raikes's departure and bought it for £1,360 in 1796; later, for a short time, he was curate of St Mary's.

The few Nicolls who lived at Neasdon in the last quarter of the 18th century were all young. In 1776 Edward Nicoll (b.1735) severed his already tenuous connexion with Neasdon by moving to Studham to take up an inheritance from the Sibleys; he married a local woman Ann Baker in 1777, held office as sheriff of Bedfordshire in 1794 and died in 1799 leaving four sons, one of whom married a young Nicoll girl at Hendon in 1803. So it was left entirely to the third generation (that is to say the children of Thomas the younger) to keep the family flag flying at Neasdon in the final quarter of the century.

In fact, neither of Thomas's two eldest sons lived at Neasdon: Thomas (b.1754) was away in the Army while John (b.1758) lived near the Mint. It was the third son Joseph (b.1761) who devoted himself to carrying on the family farming business at Neasdon which had been so dear to his father's heart. From 1782, when he came of age, Joseph farmed Neasdon Farm and Wilson's (now generally known as Brewer's after a recent tenant) and later he took on Norman's after Christopher Higgins. But in 1780 he was still only 19 and for once the name Nicoll does not appear at all in the list of farming tenancies for that year. Of Joseph's younger brothers Edward (b.1762) went to live at the Hyde while William (b.1766) moved to Harlesden, where he farmed over 150 acres, renting incidentally a small piece of land called the 'parish close' on the north side of the old Harrow road (later Craven park).

Nonetheless the Nicoll family were still strongly represented in Neasdon in 1780, though under another name. In the 1740s Joseph Finch, a member of a Harlesden family which was sufficiently notable to have a coat of arms with the motto 'carpe diem', had married Elizabeth daughter of William Coomes of the Hyde, Hendon. In 1772 their youngest son Joseph (b.1749) married his cousin Susanna Nicoll (b.1751) eldest daughter of Thomas Nicoll the younger and his wife Mary Coomes, Elizabeth's sister. In late 1772 or early 1773 the newlyweds Joseph and Susanna Finch moved into Dolley's hill farm, in which the Nicoll family had a one-fifth interest, in succession to Francis Page who had been there for about thirty years and was frequently one of the

Willesden parish churchwardens, sometimes in tandem with Joseph Finch the elder of Harlesden. Young Joseph Finch was thus handily situated to take on Neasdon Farm, Turner's and the Broadfield while his brother-in-law Joseph Nicoll was still a minor. He also acquired in 1780 about 18 acres of land bordering the west side of the Neasdon-to-Kingsbury road called Upper and Lower Burgines which were to remain Finch property for about a century; and he retained for some thirty years the tenancy of Turner's and the Broadfield which adjoined his Dolley's hill property.

Inevitably the Nicoll family did not display in the last quarter of the 18th century the sort of dynamism which had flowed from Thomas the elder and Thomas the younger in the previous half-century, although the two Josephs (Nicoll and Finch) bore their share of parish office. The level of activity in the Willesden vestry seems to have suffered in consequence at least until William Nicoll, now at Harlesden, started his remarkable run of thirty years as churchwarden in 1793. Indeed one of the main contributions which Neasdon made to the parish in this period was the provision of parish dinners to meet the frequent needs of the vestrymen.

Traditionally people who performed voluntary public service were rewarded periodically with a dinner. Many charities, such as those at Wandsworth which were nourished from the hospital land at Neasdon, had the provision of an annual dinner for the managers written into their constitution and a similar tradition applied to servants of parish vestries. The earliest surviving record of a parish dinner served for the vestrymen at the Neasdon 'Dog' is dated January 1779, when Edward Davis (or Davies) was the publican and mutton cost 5d a pound. Punch was drunk freely at these dinners and liquor often accounted for half of the total bill. The examples of dinner bills quoted in Appendix V show that the publican's spelling was frequently not up to the standard of his victuals, 'vedgatables' and 'and setra' (for 'etc') being not uncommon.

It was a sleepy, perhaps complacent, parish to which Neasdon belonged at the end of the 18th century. But when the war against Napoleon was resumed after the breakdown of the Treaty of Amiens in 1803, the parish vestry at a meeting presided over by churchwarden William Nicoll came out with a declaration of patriotic resolve as sturdy as any made in 1940:

> '..The inhabitants of this district, feeling with gratitude to Providence the blessings they enjoy under a well-regulated and enviable constitution which they inherit from their ancestors and desirous of testifying to their fellow subjects their resolution to preserve the same inviolate, do declare and resolve that they will, to the utmost of their power, co-operate with all such measures as the wisdom of government shall think fit to adopt for the defence of their king, country, religion and laws against the threatened invasion and all other attacks whatsoever.'

The stimulating effect of national danger was no doubt one of the factors which led to a quite remarkable upsurge of parish activity in the first decade of the new century. But there were others, as we shall see.

PART TWO
The Half Century to 1853

A. Resurgence

THE EVENT which brought John Nicoll the moneyer back to Neasdon House and led to a reanimation both of the hamlet and of Willesden's parish vestry was the death of Susanna Nicoll of Page street, Hendon, at Bath in 1803. In her will she appointed three executors: her cousins Thomas and John (the two eldest sons of her uncle Thomas the younger of Neasdon) and her cousin-by-marriage Joseph Finch of Dolley's hill, husband of their sister Susanna. In effect the will left Copt hall and some other Hendon properties to Thomas.

Thomas Nicoll, born at Neasdon and christened in St Mary's Willesden in February 1754, had an adventurous career. He had already joined the Army at the age of 17 as an ensign in the 33rd Regiment of Foot when he came into possession of Norman's farm near the Harrow road. Soon after his promotion to lieutenant in 1775 the regiment was posted to America where the War of Independence was about to break out. The Atlantic voyage from Cork was beset by bad weather and took over three months to complete. During the war, when the regiment was frequently in action, Thomas obtained a captaincy in the 70th Regiment of Foot, later called the Surrey regiment. He sailed to Martinique with his regiment as a brevet-major in 1794 but was soon posted back to England for urgent recruiting duty to make good the heavy losses sustained from yellow fever. Such expeditions to the West Indies between 1793 and 1796 are estimated to have cost the British army 80,000 casualties, half of whom were invalided out (double the total number of British casualties in the whole of the Peninsular war of 1808–14). The experience of Thomas's regiment was typical: when it sailed back to England a year later it had only seven officers left out of twenty-two. The commanding officer, who was himself recovering from fever, was sent over to Ireland on staff duties and Thomas, now the senior major of the regiment, was effectively its commander for the next three years.

In 1798 Thomas was promoted lieutenant-colonel but next year came the bad news that there was to be a second regimental tour to the West Indies. However, the ship carrying Thomas and about half the regiment sprang a leak off Portugal and had to return home by stages. In 1802 the 70th moved to Chatham, where the garrison was commanded by Sir John Moore; and in the next year they were ordered to Shorncliffe to help in frustrating Napoleon's threatened cross-Channel invasion. Soon afterwards they had to embark once more for the dreaded West Indies, this time Antigua, where again half the officers were to perish of sickness. Thomas, however, luckily missed this expedition, becoming instead the first commander of the new second battalion of the 44th (East Essex) regiment when it was raised in Ireland in October 1803, following the breakdown five months earlier of the short-lived Treaty of Amiens; and in June 1804 he retired from Army service. Curiously he is always described subsequently as the former lieutenant-colonel of the 70th Regiment of Foot and his final appointment in the 44th is never mentioned.

It can safely be assumed that Thomas's retirement from the Army in 1804 was connected with the responsibilities at Hendon given to him by Susanna Nicoll's will. He was formally admitted to his Hendon inheritance at a meeting of the Hendon manor court in May 1804, and in 1805 he married Sarah Geeves, a woman twenty years younger than himself whose father William had been the tenant farmer on Susanna's land. Sarah died childless in 1806. Two years later Thomas married Catherine Clarke Lewis, who was even younger than his first wife, being fully thirty years his junior.

At the ripe age of 55 Thomas started his family at Copt hall. His first son Thomas was born in 1809, a second son William in 1810, a third son John in 1813 and finally a daughter Catherine Maria in 1819 when her father was then turned 65. When he died at Copt hall in 1824 Thomas naturally left his estate to his wife and children, but within ten years his son John died at the age of 13 and his widow in 1834 aged 50.

Meanwhile John Nicoll the moneyer, who also had responsibilities under Susanna's will, had returned to Neasdon House in 1804, enlarging the contribution made by his family to the local affairs of Neasdon and Willesden. His younger brother William Nicoll, now of Harlesden, was already so firmly established as one of the two churchwardens of the parish that his re-election from year to year was almost a formality; and when the vicar was unable to preside at the vestry it was normally William who took the chair. In the previous century a Nicoll had invariably been one of the two assessors who assessed each year how the land tax quota for the parish should be apportioned locally and this tradition carried over into the new century.

The first sign that the return of John Nicoll and the arrival of James Hall at the Grove in 1806 had imparted a new vigour to the parish was when the Vestry set up a committee, near the end of 1807, to examine the case for having a resident curate at St Mary's. The committee, which consisted of Joseph Finch, William Sellon of Harlesden, Peter White of Brondesbury, James Hall, John Nicoll and William Nicoll, reported in favour of the idea, recommending that an annual collection from the ratepayers should provide the necessary finance. The aim of the annual 'vicar's collection', as it was later called, was to raise over £100 in accordance with a list of assessments expressed in multiples and fractions of a guinea and based, like the parish rates, on rateable value. As the money was to be collected 'by William Nicoll each year' it was evidently assumed that William would be willing and able to do this job indefinitely. The assumption was not ill-founded: William continued to serve faithfully year after year as churchwarden and laid down the burden only when he moved to Amersham in 1823.

Encouraged by its success in establishing the residential curacy, the Vestry now moved into the field of education. It was over thirty years since Richard Freelove, born apparently in Willesden in 1695, had died in Hendon in 1776 leaving behind him £200 for assisting the creation in Willesden of a charity school for teaching poor children to read. He also left £10 'to be laid out in bread and distributed as the Minister and churchwardens shall think fit.'

The idea of having a Willesden school was possibly inspired by the existence of a school of a different kind which the Rev. Raikes started at Neasdon some time after his arrival in 1774. It did not originate with Freelove, whose bequest was to be a contribution towards something which had 'been proposed some time since', and the money was to be paid over within four years of his death if and when the school was 'likely to be established'. Within the next year or two the Willesden vestry set up a body of four trustees to handle the legacy, consisting of the vicar (the Rev. Moses Wight), John Nicoll the lawyer, John Haley and Joseph Finch. Armed with plans to build a schoolroom, the trustees evidently applied for and obtained the money. But as Freelove had well understood, his £200 might be sufficient to buy the land and put up a building but would leave little over for meeting the running costs, which would have to be met by the ratepayers. Had the parish possessed in the last quarter of the 18th century public-spirited men of the calibre of the two Thomas Nicolls, quicker progress would doubtless have been made. But the necessary drive was lacking. The money left over after the erection of the schoolroom was invested to await a more favourable time; and it was to be a whole generation before the next steps were taken, after James Hall acquired the Neasdon property where Raikes had had his school.

In December 1809, two years after setting up the committee on the residential curacy, the Vestry resolved to start a Sunday school for the poor children of the parish, using the schoolroom at Church End. A meeting attended by the curate (the Rev. J. Griffin), William Sellon, John Nicoll, James Hall, Mr Moore and Mr Hawkins set up an association called The Subscribers and appointed a committee consisting of the curate (who was also the treasurer), the churchwardens and six others. It is evident from the proceedings of the committee and of the full association, which met once a quarter, that the leaders of the enterprise were the curate, Hall and Nicoll. For a time in 1811 and during later periods when there was no curate James Hall acted as treasurer and chaired the meetings, while John Nicoll took the lead in the annual scrutiny of the accounts.

After a school master and mistress had been appointed, the number of pupils admitted to the school quickly rose to over a hundred. The children, who had to come 'clean, washed and combed', received instruction in the schoolroom from 9 a.m. to 10.45 a.m., attended morning service in the church (where they sat in the gallery) and then had further school instruction until 1 o'clock. As the tuition was primarily for the children of the poor there were no fees. In fact the school provided some children with items of clothing but pupils could be expelled for repeatedly 'lying, swearing, pilfering, talking in an indecent manner or otherwise misbehaving'. Initially the maximum age for boy pupils was twelve and for girls thirteen but these maxima were increased slightly later on. Naturally Neasdon children attended the school along with the rest but the records show that they never accounted for more than a tenth of the total enrolment.

JOHN NICOLL of NEASDON (1758-1819); Fellow of the Company of Moneyers at the Royal Mint

The main source of income was the subscriptions made in terms of guineas by The Subscribers. There were also donations from absentee landlords like Lord Temple, All Souls College and the deans and chapters of St Paul's and Westminster, which together accounted for about a fifth of the annual income, while a further fifth came from the collection taken at an annual service in St Mary's at which a visiting preacher gave a 'charity sermon'. Finally there was the income from the Freelove money invested in a holding of £200 in 3% Consols in the names of the four Freelove trustees (Joseph Finch, Joseph Nicoll, William Nicoll, Peter White) but this never came to more than a tenth of the annual income from all sources.

From the outset the Subscribers collected an annual amount well in excess of the level of expenditure, presumably with the aim of building up a reserve for expanding the school's activities later; and in 1813 a further £100 of Consols were bought for a purchase cost of about £60 in the names not of the Freelove trustees but of the curate (the Rev. W.T. Say), William Sellon and John Nicoll. Subsequently the interest from the new £100 Consols was described in the accounts as being 'by Mr John Nicoll' whereas the income from the Freelove money was 'by Mr William Nicoll'.

By mid-1818, eight years after starting the Sunday school, the Vestry felt able to extend the school's activities to weekdays. At the quarterly meeting of the Subscribers in August the three members present (Nicoll, Hall and the curate, the Rev. T.S. Woodman) decided that school hours for Mondays to Fridays should be 9 o'clock to noon in the morning and 2 o'clock to 5 in the afternoon (1 o'clock to 3 in winter), with no school on Saturdays; holidays were limited to a week at Christmas, three days at Easter and a fortnight in the summer at harvest time. In 1821 there were 116 pupils in the school and it was decided to have a separate room for the boys in the form of a second storey to the schoolhouse. The cost of this enlargement was defrayed out of the £100 of Consols which were sold in 1822 for £76.12.6, representing a capital gain of over £16 compared with their purchase cost in 1813. Nevertheless, there was a small deficit in the accounts for the first time at the end of 1822, which led to a decision to introduce 'children's pence' in mid-1823 at the rate of a penny a week per child, to be paid each Monday morning.

Besides the start of the Sunday school the year 1810 had seen the setting up of numerous Vestry committees on such matters as altering the gallery in the church (where the Sunday school children were to sit during morning service), improving church paths, getting an organ installed in the church and drawing up rules for a parish benefit society. In these committees the names of certain activists appeared frequently and none more regularly than those of Nicoll and Hall of Neasdon.

Of particular long-term importance was a motion proposed at the Vestry in 1812 by Hall and seconded by Nicoll to set up a committee to examine and register the parish charities as required by a recent Act of Parliament. The labours of this committee, which included the curate, the churchwardens, Nicoll, Hall and two others, led to the drawing up of a new list of ten trustees in 1813 to handle the Neasdon House charities. The list contained no fewer than four of the Nicoll family and two of their relations the Finches.* Twenty years later James Hall's was the only Neasdon name in the new list of 1834.

It was in 1810 or thereabouts that Neasdon felt the first impact of the claims of commercial transport which were to play such a big part in its later development. In the 1790s the Grand Junction canal was constructed linking the canal system of the midlands with the Thames and in 1801 a 'Paddington arm' of the canal was opened running from the main canal near Uxbridge to Paddington basin (later called Little Venice). The idea of a further canal running eastwards from the Paddington basin to reach the Thames at Limehouse began to emerge late in 1802.

Water supply was always a major problem for canals and an obvious source for the Paddington arm was the river Brent which it crossed some two miles west of Neasdon near Twyford. The idea of a Brent reservoir opposite Kingsbury was considered in 1803 but deferred. A similar fate was suffered in the following year by the simpler

**see Appendix III, a*

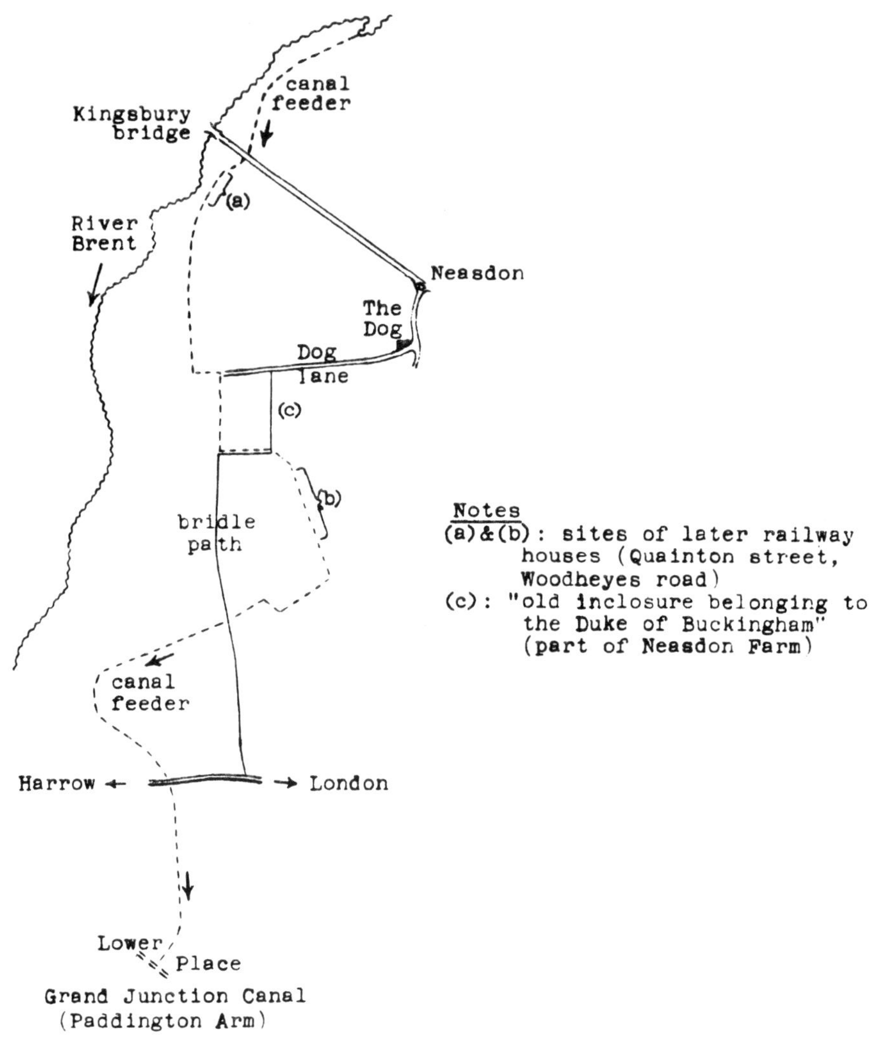

proposal to construct a feeder from the Brent in north Neasdon to run for 3¼ miles through Neasdon Bottom before reaching the Paddington arm of the canal beyond Harrow road at Lower Place near Harlesden. Eventually the feeder plan got the go-ahead in 1809, the necessary strips of land were bought from the various landowners concerned and construction was put in hand without further delay.[14] The feeder left the river at a point where the hospital land formed the south bank and where it could serve as an outlet from a Brent reservoir should one be built later. It then ran in some places along the old boundary lines between enclosed estates, making some right-angle turns, and for a short distance alongside Dog lane.

Shortly afterwards the Regent's Canal Company got authority to build the Regent's canal from Paddington to Limehouse, which was completed by stages and opened in full in 1820. The case for a Brent reservoir was now stronger. In the 1830s a reservoir was constructed which covered 69 acres, including some 14 acres of the hospital land, and cost over £11,000. Thanks to the foresight exercised earlier, the existing feeder at Neasdon needed only slight adjustment.

More complicated adjustments to Neasdon land resulted from the Enclosure Award made in 1823 by commissioners appointed under the Willesden Enclosure Act of 1815. Considerable areas of common land such as Neasdon field (near the Brent), Brent field and Dudding hill field were awarded to owners of neighbouring lands and enclosed. At the same time many strips of waste land at the side of the roads, which had been useful to carts and carriages wishing to pass other vehicles or to avoid floods and ruts in the centre of the road, were incorporated into adjoining fields and fenced in. For instance the dean and chapter of Westminster got several acres of land to the west of the road leading to Kingsbury bridge and also a strip of land in front of their cottage, later called Neasdon Cottage, which was sited next to Neasdon Farm across the road from Neasdon House. Also enclosed near the Neasdon end of Dolley's hill road was an old track, marked on Rocque's map of 1746 and known later as Scotch lane, which ran down to Sherrick green. This lane was ordered to be incorporated into the two fields along whose western edge it ran, called Bowling-alley field and (higher up) Sheephouse field, which also gained a piece of open land which stood between the mouth of the lane and the road to Dolley's hill.

The Enclosure documents show how people thought of the roads round Neasdon at that time. There was 'Dolley's hill road' and 'Dudden hill road' but there was no short title for the later Neasdon lane, which was referred to rather clumsily as 'the Church End to Kingsbury Bridge road'. In legal documents and in conversation the description of a road no doubt varied according to where the person describing it was standing. A Neasdon man would probably have talked of 'Church road' in one direction and 'Kingsbury road' in the other; and 'Kingsbury road' in fact appears on a map drawn for the Duke of Chandos in 1787. The general width prescribed for these country roads was 30 feet, except where old enclosures made them narrower. Exceptionally, near the crossroads at Neasdon the landowners John Nicoll and James Hall voluntarily surrendered strips of land to allow a road width of 40 feet; and this and later widenings at the road junction gradually ate into the grass triangle known as Neasdon green.

Dog lane, named after the 'Dog' public house at its Neasdon end but known earlier as Stones lane, formed the first part of a 1¾-mile path to Harlesden which is described as follows in the Enclosure Award:-

'One other private occupation road and public bridleway and footway of the breadth of 20 feet branching out of the Harrow turnpike road... and proceeding in a northwardly direction through Upper Brent field to the culvert on the public drain and from there in the same direction in a straight line towards the Grand Junction

Canal feeder and turning in an easterly direction along the south side of the said feeder to an old inclosure belonging to the Duke of Buckingham and thence in a northwardly direction in its present track over the said feeder it enters an old lane called Dog lane and thence in an easterly direction along the said lane until it enters the public highway called the Church End and Kingsbury Bridge road at or near a certain public house called the Dog in Neasdon'.

The 'old inclosure belonging to the Duke of Buckingham' lay south of Dog lane and belonged to Neasdon Farm. After Margaret Nicoll had died childless in 1768 James Brydges, Marquis of Carnarvon and later Duke of Chandos, had a daughter by his second wife whose husband Earl Temple was successively Marquis of Buckingham and Duke of Buckingham-and-Chandos. In the early 19th century the Brydges family started shedding some of their land in Willesden, notably at Dolley's hill and Oxgate, and in 1818 John Nicoll took the first steps towards acquiring from them their 60% share of Neasdon House and of Wilson's (Brewer's) farm and their 50% share in Turner's. Eventually Neasdon Farm also passed into Nicoll ownership, but this was many years after the death of John Nicoll the moneyer in 1819.

John the moneyer was the first of the Neasdon Nicolls to be buried in the churchyard of St Mary's Willesden, a whole century after his grandfather Thomas the elder arrived in the parish. He left his property in the first instance to his wife Elizabeth, who carried on dispensing the Neasdon House 'coal money' and subscribing to the school until her death in 1828, when under the terms of John's will the estate passed to their nephew Joseph, who had joined the Royal Mint under his uncle's tutelage in 1804.

As had happened half a century earlier, several deaths now occurred in the Nicoll family within the space of a few years. Joseph Nicoll the farmer (b. 1761) who had married an Elizabeth Nicoll (her maiden name) from the Hyde and was the father of Joseph the moneyer (b. 1788), Ann (b. 1792), John (b. 1795) and Thomas (b. 1798), died in 1823 and his wife in 1830. In 1823, too, Joseph Finch died at Dolley's hill, having outlived his wife Susanna by twenty years; and in the next year or two the new Dolley's hill house was built by his successor. Joseph Finch had had a large family including a son Robert (b. 1789) who was apprenticed at the Mint soon after Joseph Nicoll, doubtless under the same sponsor John Nicoll. So for a considerable part of the first quarter of the new century the Nicolls and Finches had no fewer than three representatives at the Royal Mint at the same time. To understand what lay behind this we need to take a closer look at the business of manufacturing the coin of the realm on Tower Hill.

B: Moneying at the Mint

For centuries before the Nicolls came to Neasdon the Guild or Company of Moneyers had had the job of converting bullion into the coins required by the king and his officials.[15] In the 18th century the company operated under a contract negotiated between their provost (leader) and the Master of the Mint (who at the start of the century was Sir Isaac Newton) with payment on a piece-rate basis. So when any innovation was made in the coinage system the company had plenty of work to do, making large profits which were shared out among the 'fellows' according to rules devised by themselves. But in some years the Treasury needed no new coins and then the moneyers would have had no income if there had not been a longstanding arrangement under which a salary was payable to each moneyer when the value of the coins minted in the year fell below a certain level. In the quaint language of 1729 this was so as 'not to suffer them to be too far exposed to temptation by their Necessities'.

The Company was self-recruited. A member was allowed, subject to the approval of the Master, to introduce an apprentice who after seven years' training became a fellow. A fellow sponsoring an apprentice had the duty of instructing him and generally looking after him during the apprenticeship. By the 19th century the entry fee for an apprentice on being bound had risen to £1,000, while on promotion to fellow he contributed a further £500 to the company's capital, though it remained legally his and was payable to his estate when he died.

Such a company tended in time to become something of a collective family business. A list compiled soon after 1700 includes fifteen moneyers, including the provost, and nine apprentices of whom probably three and possibly five were moneyers' sons. Several in the list were of Hendon origin, notably John Braint the provost, and the provostship was to rest in Hendon hands for most of the century. In 1742 when Henry Haley was provost there were nine fellows, including John Haley the brother of Susan Nicoll, but there was no Nicoll at that time, though there had been two 'Nicolls' in the list forty years earlier. It was without doubt Susan's brother who took on her son Joseph as his apprentice in about 1745 – the first of three generations of Neasdon moneyers.

The Nicoll succession at Neasdon House
and in the Company of Moneyers at the Royal Mint

At Neasdon House (owner or part-owner)	Thomas Nicoll d.1772	Joseph Nicoll d.1773	John Nicoll d.1782	John Nicoll d.1819	Elizabeth Nicoll d.1828	Joseph Nicoll d.1853
At the Royal Mint: year of entry	—	?1745	—	1774	—	1804
relation to predecessor	—	nephew	—	nephew	—	nephew

Families of the Dollis hill ridge at the Royal Mint.

(moneyers' names in capitals)

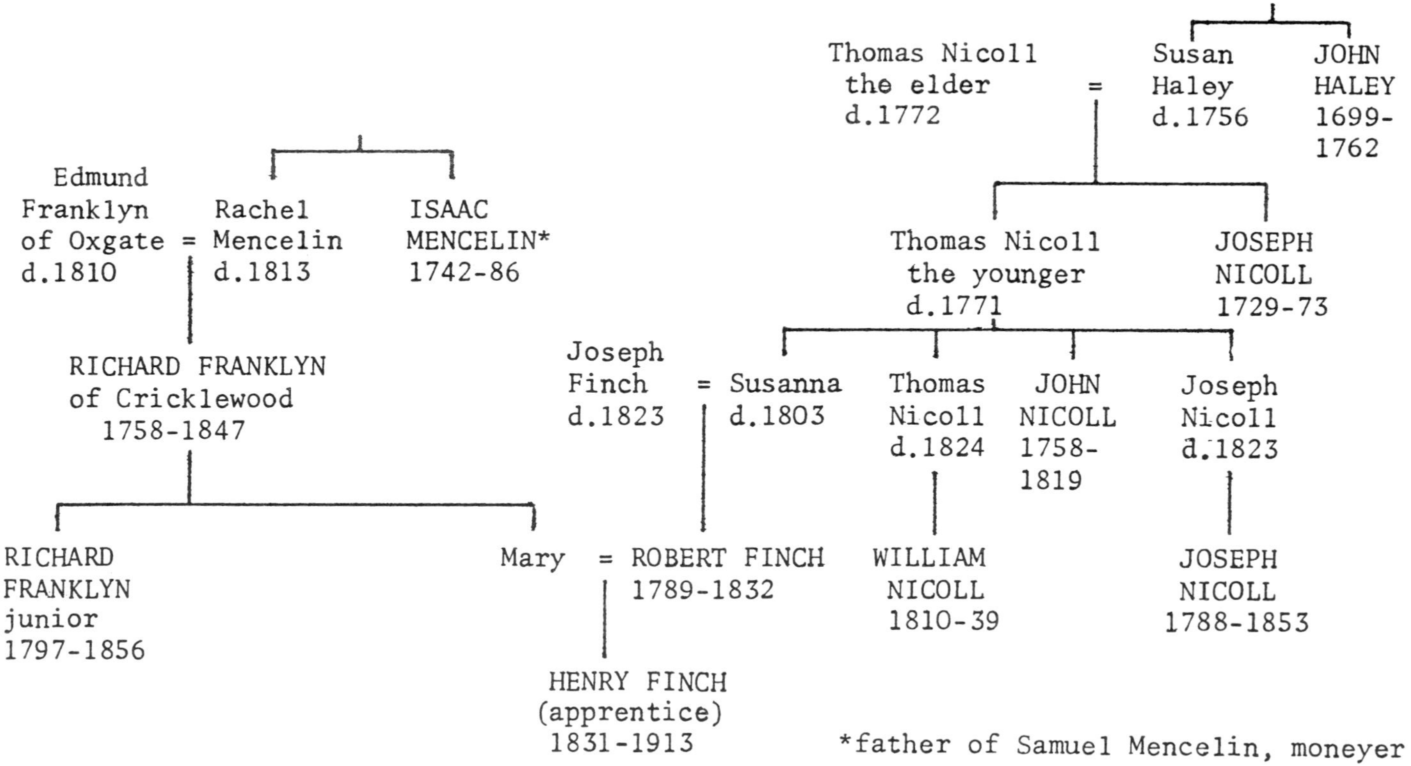

Edmund Franklyn of Oxgate d.1810 = Rachel Mencelin d.1813

Rachel Mencelin d.1813; ISAAC MENCELIN* 1742-86

RICHARD FRANKLYN of Cricklewood 1758-1847

RICHARD FRANKLYN junior 1797-1856; Mary

Thomas Nicoll the elder d.1772 = Susan Haley d.1756

Susan Haley d.1756; JOHN HALEY 1699-1762

Thomas Nicoll the younger d.1771; JOSEPH NICOLL 1729-73

Joseph Finch d.1823 = Susanna d.1803

Susanna d.1803; Thomas Nicoll d.1824; JOHN NICOLL 1758-1819; Joseph Nicoll d.1823

Mary = ROBERT FINCH 1789-1832

WILLIAM NICOLL 1810-39

JOSEPH NICOLL 1788-1853

HENRY FINCH (apprentice) 1831-1913

*father of Samuel Mencelin, moneyer

Joseph Nicoll indirectly bequeathed his interest in Neasdon House to his nephew John (b. 1758) but any plans he may have had to make John his apprentice at the Mint were interrupted by his own early death at only 43 early in 1773. However, on 20 January 1774 the Master of the Mint gave permission for both John Nicoll and Richard Franklyn (son of Edmund Franklyn of Oxgate and nephew of the moneyer Isaac Mencelin) to be bound apprentice to the company. Similarly John Nicoll in turn took his nephew Joseph (b. 1788) as his apprentice in 1804 and Joseph, again, inherited Neasdon House. So there must be a very strong presumption that when Joseph Nicoll in 1827 took as his apprentice his cousin William, the lieutenant-colonel's son from Copt hall, Hendon, there was a future foreseen for William at Neasdon House. This presumption is powerfully reinforced by the fact that William stopped living at Hendon and made his home with his unmarried cousin as 'William Nicoll of the Royal Mint and of Neasdon'. But the plan misfired. William died at Neasdon House in 1839, leaving a widow but no children, and was taken back to Hendon for interment in the vault for the Copt hall Nicolls. And Joseph had to rethink his plans for Neasdon House.

The residents of Neasdon House were not the only people in north Willesden to be in the moneying business at the Mint. On Dolley's hill Robert Finch (1789–1832), one of the many sons of Joseph Finch and Susanna Nicoll, started an apprenticeship in 1805. Richard Franklyn of Oxgate (b. 1758) had begun at the Mint under the care of his uncle Isaac Mencelin (b. 1742) and became provost in 1834 at the age of 75. His son Richard Franklyn junior (b. 1797) followed in his father's steps at the Mint and in 1820 his sister Mary married the moneyer Robert Finch in St Mary's Willesden. Isaac Mencelin who died at Cricklewood in the parish of Hendon in 1786, Richard Franklyn senior who died aged 88 at Totteridge in 1847 and Richard Franklyn junior who died in Suffolk in 1856 all 'came home' to Willesden parish church to be buried. Robert Finch's son Henry (1831–1913) began his apprenticeship at the Mint in 1846 but had not completed his seven-year term of tuition when the system was changed. So strongly were these three allied families from the Dolley's hill ridge – the Nicolls of Neasdon, the Franklyns of Oxgate and Cricklewood, and the Finches of Dolley's hill – represented at the Royal Mint in the first half of the 19th century that, taking the period as a whole, they accounted for half the total membership of the company. Five of these moneyers were buried in Willesden churchyard between 1819 and 1856.

One of the engaging traditions of the moneyers was that when they wrote their wills they would leave a small legacy to each of their fellow-moneyers. Thus Joseph Nicoll (d. 1773) left 'to my brother Moneyers at His Majesty's Mint within the Tower of London one gold ring of the value of one guinea'; and John Haley (d. 1762), Isaac Mencelin (d. 1786) and W.W. Van der Esch (d. 1789) did exactly the same. A generation later the moneyers were more affluent and in 1819, by which time the Mint was housed in a separate new building on Tower Hill outside the Tower itself, we find John Nicoll leaving 'to the Provost and each of my brother Moneyers five guineas for a ring as a small token of my regard for them'. Robert Finch in 1832 bequeathed 'to each of the Moneyers of His Majesty's Mint the sum of £10' while in 1847 Richard Franklyn the provost left 'to each member of the chartered Company of Moneyers of

Her Majesty's Mint a gold mourning ring of such value as my executrix and executors shall think proper'.

The traditional system of moneying at the Mint began to be questioned after the reissue of the gold coinage which started in 1774. This involved a great deal of work for the moneyers and thanks to the piece-rate method of remuneration they made very large profits. In 1782 the Treasury got two consultants to look at the Mint and its methods, but nothing of significance happened as a result of their report. In 1836, however, a parliamentary select committee was appointed which took voluminous evidence from the Mint officers and the leading moneyers, only for the whole operation to be stopped by a dissolution of Parliament.

At the time of the inquiry, whose records survive in printed form, the provost of the moneyers was Richard Franklyn senior, an old man of nearly 80, having succeeded the octogenarian Henry Atkinson who died in harness in 1834. In fact the moneyers were never superannuated, even though they might become unfit for duty, and they continued to share annually in the profit distribution while they lived. The spokesman for the moneyers at the inquiry was in fact Jasper Atkinson a 'senior moneyer' who was the son of the former provost and related to the former moneyer W.W. Van der Esch (who was himself the son of a former deputy Master). He explained during his evidence that the paralysis which afflicted Joseph Nicoll (his exact contemporary at the Mint) made him unfit for duty. Also mentioned in the hearings was William Nicoll, who was described as 'a cousin of one of the moneyers' (this would be Joseph) and 'nephew of one now dead' (this would be John, d. 1819).

It is important to note that this tradition of keeping membership of the company largely within a few moneying families was acknowledged to be in the public interest. The clipping and counterfeiting of coins brought a steady stream of offenders before the courts and a report by the Master of the Mint and others quoted by a parliamentary committee of finance in 1797 said of the moneyers

> 'that any casual Coinage of Money given to other Individuals will serve to initiate Workmen in the Art for a Time and then afterwards most probably leave them to practise it, to the great Detriment of the Public, by counterfeiting the Coins'.

Recruits to the company were required to take an oath before the Master or his deputy not to reveal the technological secrets of the Mint.[16] The company itself encouraged loyalty and probity among its members by the initial down-payment and by dealing severely with offenders, sometimes expelling them from the company, with the consent of the Master, and barring them permanently from re-entry.

In 1846 the Government set up a Royal Commission to look at the Mint and make recommendations. The Commission went thoroughly into the history of moneying at the Mint. For the moneyers evidence was given by the provost Sir Jasper Atkinson and by Richard Franklyn junior as one of the 'senior moneyers'. Joseph Nicoll was in fact now the most senior of the moneyers but it was explained that for health reasons he rarely attended for duty at the Mint. The company of moneyers resolutely refused, as in the previous inquiry, to submit their books for examination but it was established beyond dispute that in the years of the great recoinage of gold coins in the 1770s each moneyer made over £2,000 a year clear profit and that by the 1840s a typical annual profit for a moneyer had risen to about £3,000. The chief reason for this increase was not inflation but advances in manufacturing technology which allowed the number of fellows to decline from fifteen in 1706 to nine in 1760 and an average of six in the next century. It was also agreed that the moneyers had 'in great measure confined the company to their own relations'.

One of the recommendations of the Royal Commission when it reported in 1849 was that everyone at the Mint should be salaried and that all contracting should cease. This meant that after a short period the Company of the Moneyers would be dissolved. The moneyers accepted their fate but submitted a memorial to the Government in 1851 about their severance terms, pointing to their length of devoted service and to the financial investment they had all made in the company. The Treasury responded in a Minute offering annual pensions of £1,000 each to Sir Jasper Atkinson and Joseph Nicoll and of £900 to Richard Franklyn. The more junior moneyers and the apprentices were offered salaried posts but when none of them accepted they too received annual pensions: Edward Enfield (exceptionally a protégé of the Master) and Robert Rentoul (Atkinson's nephew) got £600 and £500 a year respectively while the apprentices Henry Finch and F.R. Brande, who had each paid his £1,000 entrance fee on being bound but had so far received only the daily allowance as reward, got £150 a year each.

When the 'Company and Fellowship of the Moneyers' was dissolved in the summer of 1851 it sold to Joseph Nicoll under its common seal a built-up estate at Hoxton (Hackney) called The Moneyers Land. The freehold of this land, which contained several streets of houses, including Provost street and Moneyer street and a public house called The Moneyers Arms, remained in Joseph's family until after the 1914 war.

C: The Neasdon House Pew

While doubts about the future of moneying at the Mint must have troubled the mind of Joseph Nicoll from the 1830s onwards, there were problems nearer home, affecting his place in the local Willesden community, which caused feelings to run ever more deeply as time went by.

The deaths among the Nicoll family in 1819–23 had inevitably reduced the part they now played in Willesden affairs at the Vestry; but their influence remained for a time substantial. On the four-man board of Freelove trustees Joseph Nicoll and Robert Finch the moneyers were appointed in 1826 to succeed their deceased fathers, while William Nicoll's place was taken by James Hall in 1831 and after him by his elder son Henry Hall in 1839.

The Roberts charities continued to be dispensed from Neasdon House first by Elizabeth Nicoll (d. 1828) and later by Joseph, but it is not clear what the role of the Vestry was in the nomination of the necessary ten trustees. The method laid down for nominating new trustees was that this should be done by the survivors from the previous list, but when there was a break in continuity the owner of Neasdon House traditionally took action. It is not clear whether the list of 1813 was drawn up by the Vestry on its own supposed authority or whether it should be regarded as John Nicoll's list drawn up with Vestry advice. A background note prepared by the solicitor James Hall in 1833 implies that in his view responsibility for the new nominations in 1834 should rest with the survivors of the 1767 list or with their eldest sons, which suggests that Hall may have forgotten the existence of the 1813 list, although his own name was included in it. What actually happened in 1834 was that the new list of ten recorded in the Vestry minute book contained neither Richard Franklyn nor Joseph Nicoll, although both were survivors from the 1813 list.* This apparent irregularity is not easy to explain; nor do we know what view Joseph Nicoll took of the matter or what part it may have played in the later souring of relations betwen Joseph and the Vestry. The chief reason, however, for the long estrangement of Neasdon House from the Vestry over the next half-century was undoubtedly the Neasdon House pew in the church.

Among the badges of rank symbolizing the place of Neasdon House in the local community none was more visible to people generally than the pew reserved for the occupier of the house in St Mary's church, which lay midway between Neasdon and Harlesden. There the Roberts family established in the 16th century a large box-type pew, bearing the family crest, for their use at divine service. The pew seems to have stood 4½ feet high on the south side of the chancel at the end of the nave, preventing those behind it from seeing the chancel or the altar except when standing. This did not matter much as long as the congregation was small but as the parish population grew so did the problem.

For a long time the state of the church had been causing concern. The building suffered badly from damp, chiefly because of the lowlying ground on which it stood, and it was thought that the walls, which were surrounded by an earthbank, would need substantial reconstruction. Another problem was the inadequacy of the seating arrangements, noted as early as 1824. In March 1843 the Vestry resolved

> 'that the church be re-pewed and made as comfortable as possible to accommodate numerous families now without sittings'

and also

> 'that a Church Rate be made at the rate of 2d in the pound for the repair of the church and re-pewing it'.

The Vestry were aware however that they might not have an entirely free hand to change the existing seating. So they further resolved

> 'that the Vestry Clerk prepare a case and submit the same to Dr Lushington as to the rights of the dean and chapter of St Paul's to the seats in the chancel and of Mr Joseph Nicoll and Mr Hall to three seats in the body of the church and as to the course the Parish should take in reference thereto in the projected re-pewing of the church'.[17]

The Neasdon House pew was not the only one involved. A right to a pew measuring twelve feet by four feet was evidently granted by faculty in 1737 to Charles Rambouillet whose family continued to own the Grove until the closing years of the

**see Appendix III, a*

18th century, latterly under the name of Cookson. After a period of ownership by the Rev. Bristow, the Grove passed in 1806 to James Hall, who five years later converted a range of outbuildings into a cottage and moved into it. Hall continued to occupy the pew in the church, although he had let the Grove to a tenant, and he seems to have done any necessary repairs to it himself.

The pew was not mentioned in the record of the sale of the Grove by the Rambouillet family in 1796 but when Hall bought the house in 1806 it was said to have 'two pews in the church against the south wall and next to the chancel'. Another transaction in 1817 involving a William Langley contains the same phrase; but the evidence presented in the 1843 submission suggests that from 1822 the two pews stood end to end against the south wall, access to the one that had been moved being through the one originally there.

The opinion of learned counsel at Doctors' Commons was given not by Dr Lushington but by a Dr Adams, who opined that Hall could not sustain a claim even to one of these pews for the Grove, let alone two. But about the Neasdon House pew he said

> 'As to Mr Nicoll the case is different. It seems to me highly probable, at the least, that he could successfully maintain a prescriptive right to his pew.'

and his conclusion was:

> 'I accordingly think that in re-pewing the church the churchwardens are no further bound to consult Mr Hall's convenience than in mere courtesy. I think that they are bound to consult Mr Nicoll; and thus they ought not to attempt to re-pew the church – nor would, or ought, the ordinary to grant them a faculty for so doing – without his being secured equal accommodation (i.e. a pew equal in size and situation), after the re-pewing of the church, [to that] which he now has or enjoys in it.'

This opinion was not at all what the Vestry wanted to hear. The pew question now fades from the record until 1847 when their architect advised a Vestry committee that

> 'from the dilapidated state of the walls and the dangerous state of the tower, the most economic plan by far would be to pull down the present church and to erect an entire new one in preference to laying out a large sum in re-pewing the present one.'

Observing that to repair the existing building would cost £1,250 whereas rebuilding the whole church with more sittings would cost no more than £2,000, the committee reached the conclusion, which they knew would startle the parishioners, that the church should be entirely rebuilt on a better site. They added that they understood the dean and chapter of St Paul's (the 'impropriators' of the existing chancel) to be willing to foot the bill for the new chancel while the Church Building Society would meet a third of the cost of any extra free sittings. The remainder of the money would come from loans raised by the parish on the security of the rates, as allowed by the Church Building Acts; for example, such loans could be repaid over a period of twenty years by means of a church rate of a penny a year. However, the full Vestry at a meeting a month later rejected their committee's recommendation by 118 votes to 52, and the church had to think again.*

**see Appendix VI*

But now the thinking could no longer be done at leisure because within a few weeks a strongly worded letter arrived from the Archdeacon of Middlesex insisting that something must be done about the dilapidation of the church to make it usable for services. Early in 1848 the Vestry set up another committee consisting of the vicar, the churchwardens and about a dozen others including Joseph Nicoll and Henry Hall. A notable feature of this list as recorded in the Vestry minutes is that Joseph Nicoll's name was given pride of place immediately after the vicar and churchwardens and before that of Lord Ernest Bruce M.P. Given the divergence of views among its members it was predictable that this committee would achieve little and in 1849 another was set up without Joseph Nicoll. In May 1850 the committee reported, recommending a plan which would make available 120 extra sittings and towards which the dean and chapter of St Paul's had undertaken to give over £200 for repairs to the chancel. The Vestry approved the new plan and gave authority for the sealing of the necessary faculty.

The parish authorities evidently thought that despite the adverse legal opinion of 1843 they had a persuasive case to put before an ecclesiastical court. The parish had a growing population of about 3,000 and its church should therefore, according to a recognised rule of thumb, have seats for 1,000 people; so, allowing for the availability of other places of worship in the southern parts of the parish, about 650 seats were

The NEASDEN HOUSE PEW *(on the right, opposite the pulpit) in St Mary's church Willesden*

needed in St Mary's - nearly double the existing number. In fact the new plan allowed for a total of about 450 seats.

To this plan both the bishop of the diocese and the St Paul's authorities gave their consent. It remained only to persuade the Bishop of London's Consistory Court that the general interest should be put above the archaic privileges of Neasdon House. In an attempt to coax Joseph Nicoll into an agreement the Vestry offered to erect in the same position in the church a new Neasdon House pew large enough for eight persons to replace the existing one which had room for fourteen. A bachelor like Joseph, residing generally alone and seldom attending church services, could hardly (they thought) call this offer unreasonable. But reject it he did; and his own counter-offer of £50 towards the cost of repairing and re-pewing the church, provided his own pew was left untouched, brought no response from the other side.

The deadlock continued after the death in July 1850 of the vicar the Rev H.J. Knapp who was, like his predecessor, sub-dean of St Paul's. Delay in appointing a successor to Knapp held things up and it was not until April 1851 that the case came up before the consistory court. By good fortune a fairly full account of this case and others was published a year or two later by Dr J.E.P. Robertson.[18] For Joseph Nicoll it was argued that any faculty to re-pew the church should leave the Neasdon House pew untouched, on the following grounds:-

> 'That in the year 1819 Mr Nicoll became possessed of a mansionhouse and lands, with appurtenances, in the parish of Willesden, called Neasdon House, and that he and his lessees have ever since occupied that house and enjoyed the use of a certain pew in the parish church as appurtenant thereto. That the said mansionhouse etc came in the year 1743 from the heirs and assignees of Sir William Roberts into the possession of Mr Nicoll's ancestors who have ever since 1743 occupied the house and constantly used and occupied the pew as appurtenant thereto, and that the pew has beyond memory been reputed and considered to be annexed and appurtenant to the said house. That the pew was in, and previously to, the year 1582 used by Edmund Roberts Esq, an ancestor of the said Sir William Roberts, both of whom were occupiers of the said house. That on a monumental tablet erected in the chancel to the memory of the said Edmund Roberts he is described [as] of Neasdon, in the said parish, and his armorial bearings are engraven thereon; that the same armorial bearings are also carved on the outside panel of the said pew, and the same bearings were likewise carved in the said mansionhouse and remained till within the last ten years. . .
>
> 'It was further alleged that Mr Nicoll from time to time since he became the occupier of the mansionhouse caused the pew and the lock to be repaired at his own cost; and especially in the year 1820 caused a new flooring to be laid down and also in the year 1840 a new seat to be fixed in the pew. It was also alleged that the pews and sittings in the church had, within the memory of divers inhabitants of the parish, been repaired, altered, rearranged and made uniform in height; but that the said pew appurtenant to Neasdon House, though differing in height from the other pews, was then left in its original state and that Mr Nicoll and his ancestors had from time to time been accustomed to keep a lock on the door and occasionally had the said pew locked up, and that on the pillar within the pew an escutcheon of two of the ancestors of Mr Nicoll had been erected without any demand on the part of the vicar

or the churchwardens for, and without payment of, the fees accustomed to be paid for setting up similar escutcheons in other parts of the church.

'It was further alleged that the said pew is not of a height to intercept the view of the reading desk or pulpit from anyone seated in any part of the church and that it will not interfere, in its present state, with the re-pewing of the church so as to deprive the parishioners of the additional sittings intended to be provided; and that the pew is no more than adequate for the mansionhouse when fully occupied.

'And, lastly, it was alleged that Mr Nicoll had offered to renovate his pew and to treat with the parish for carrying into effect their object of re-pewing the church; subject only to the condition that no alteration should be made in the size or situation of the pew, and also that the ancient fabric and woodwork of the pew should be preserved and maintained; but that the parish had declined to treat with Mr Nicoll subject to those conditions.

'Wherefore it was prayed that the Court would not grant a faculty for repairing and re-pewing the church without a special proviso that nothing contained in the faculty should empower the parish to remove, or alter, the pew appurtenant to the mansionhouse called Neasdon House; or to molest Mr Nicoll, or his successors in the same house, from the peaceable and undisturbed enjoyment and use of the said pew; and that the vicar and churchwardens be condemned in the costs of the petition.'

These claims on behalf of Joseph Nicoll were not examined in detail by the court and it is not clear what grounds he had for dating Thomas Nicoll's occupation of Neasdon House from 1743. It is clearly not true that Joseph's ancestors 'occupied the house ever since 1743' because for over two decades near the end of the 18th century, as we have seen, it was occupied by a series of tenants. It would have been more correct to say that the Nicolls had had the house as owners or part-owners, and mostly as residents, for about a century.

Among the sworn affidavits supporting Joseph's case was one by John Cheney, carpenter, who had altered other pews in the church in 1825 but not the Neasdon House pew, having been directed by Francis Pink, master carpenter, 'not to repair or in any manner alter the pew belonging to Neasdon House'. In 1845 he was employed by Joseph Nicoll of Neasdon House 'to repair the lock, which was on the door of the pew, and to ease the door and also to fasten some of the boards forming the floor of the pew which had become loose'; these repairs had been done in pursuance of directions given by Joseph Nicoll who had paid for the work.

Giving judgement, Dr Lushington sympathised with the church authorities in their difficulties but he pointed to three facts:-

a. occupants of Neasdon House had beyond memory had use and enjoyment of the pew;

b. repairs to the pew had been done at Joseph Nicoll's expense;

c. when other pews were repaired the Neasdon House pew was not touched.

In view of these facts Dr Lushington felt bound to conclude that Joseph had so far established a prima facie case that the necessary faculty for the work could only be granted with the proviso that the Neasdon House pew should be excluded from it. Regarding costs, Dr Lushington thought that Joseph should not ask for them but that if pressed he must grant them. The application was pressed, probably because Joseph's claims would not otherwise have been seen to be completely upheld, and the costs were allowed.

After the court case the new vicar the Rev. R.W. Burton ('an Irish gentleman') tried to reason with Joseph but in vain. This was not surprising as the Vestry had not acted in other matters in a way likely to win Joseph's co-operation. On Lady Day 1850 they elected Joseph as one of the two surveyors for the parish highways for 1850–51 and when a year later his accounts had not been presented the vestry clerk was instructed to attend the special sessions at Kensington to prevent them from being allowed without parish approval. They then elected Joseph, soon after the case in the consistory court, as substitute churchwarden for 1851–52 after James Wright, a major landowner in Harlesden, who had initially been elected, had claimed exemption from the office. Joseph in his turn promptly claimed exemption on the ground that he was a moneyer at the Mint – an office 'held by Royal Charter' – and therefore exempt from compulsory parish office. Joseph's claim was conceded and George Veale of Oxgate was appointed in his place.

Relations between Joseph and the Vestry were now thoroughly soured and were never again to improve. Having failed in his peace initiative, the vicar revived the idea of rebuilding the church elsewhere but preliminary enquiries about an alternative site were unsuccessful and the matter was quickly dropped. Meanwhile Joseph, wishing to proclaim publicly the rightful place of his pew in the church (and of Neasdon House in the parish) had a brass plate fixed to the pew with the words:

> 'By adjudication in the Consistory Court of the Bishop of London dated 24th April A.D. 1851 this Pew was declared to be by prescription appurtenant to Neasdon House in this parish, the residence of Joseph Nicoll, Esq.'

Twenty years later James Wright, the 'squire' of Harlesden, was to say of the pew controversy

> 'I lament that it has caused so much angry feeling in the parish. I was, to the end of his life, on friendly terms with the late Mr Nicoll and I did not think that he was properly treated with respect to this pew. The parish took the opinion of eminent counsel on the subject of the claim and the opinion was an adverse one; but still, after a resolution of the Vestry, the right was tried and the parish defeated at the expense of some £400. . . I did all in my power to prevent these proceedings and I believe from conversations which I had with Mr Nicoll that if the parish would have acknowledged his claim without litigation he would have acceded to any reasonable proposition with regard to the pew; but, as it was, he recorded – and always to my regret – his victory by a brass plate in his pew, which to this day gives offence to many who are perfectly ignorant and innocent of the origin of it.'

The reconstruction of the church took place in 1852. For another forty years, until it was at last removed in the early 1890s, the pew with its emblems continued to be a source of pride for Neasdon House and of offence to others.

D: Mid-Century Neasdon

THE YEAR 1851, when everyone was talking about the Great Exhibition in Hyde Park, was also an eventful one, as we have seen, for Neasdon. It saw the important legal judgement about the Neasdon House pew in the church and the end of the traditional moneying system at the Royal Mint. In late March the 10-year census was taken; so it is a good time to take a look at Joseph Nicoll's contemporaries at Neasdon.

With his substantial income from the Mint Joseph Nicoll was able to bring another large area of Neasdon land under Nicoll ownership. The 'Spotted Dog' and the Broadfield had been wholly owned by the family in the time of the first Thomas Nicoll, while John Nicoll (d. 1819) had bought out the Marquis of Buckingham's three-fifths shares of Neasdon House and Wilson's (Brewer's) farm and his half-share of Turner's. Now, in a third wave of acquisition, Joseph purchased from the Duke of Buckingham-and-Chandos the 150-acre Neasdon Farm which his family had occupied for over a century until his father's death in 1823. When Thomas Nicoll the younger was tenant in the 1760s he paid £130 a year rent and made some improvements at his own expense such as erecting a brick wall round the homestead; in return he was allowed to excavate gravel from the river bank and to keep the sale proceeds, but this was stopped when Thomas died. From about 1830 the farm was known as Newman's after its tenant Robert Newman, a 'postmaster' with headquarters in Regent street in London. Newman kept the tenancy for about thirty years and was enumerated here in the 1841 census along with his bailiff George Watts. Its farmhouse should probably be identified with the house described in a deed of 1743 as

> 'that new erected messuage divided into two tenements fronting the highway from Neasdon to Wilsdon church'.

In the 1851 census the farmhouse was shared by George Watts the bailiff and an attorney called William Warwick Burton of Lincoln's Inn.

Across the road, the Grove and its lands were now owned, following James Hall's death in 1838, by his two sons Henry and Cheslyn, both of them attorneys in their thirties carrying on the family law business in New Boswell court and attached, like Burton opposite, to Lincoln's Inn. At Rose cottage, formerly an outbuilding of the Grove, lived a stockbroker William Marshall who died here in 1858 and whose family were still living in the house in 1874. At the smithy was George Jackman, one of a long line of family blacksmiths. At the 'Spotted Dog' old Joseph Twyford had recently given up and Benjamin Stratford was the licensee, to be followed a few years later by William Simmonds before the Twyfords returned.

On the northern edge of Neasdon the Brent reservoir was still developing. During an unusually cold wet spell in January 1841, part of the defences gave way and the tide of water from this and other tributaries caused flooding downstream with severe damage at Brentford and some loss of life. The inquest jury felt it to be their duty

> 'to enforce upon the directors of the Regent's canal Company, in the construction of the walls of the [Kingsbury] reservoir, lately ruptured by the ice and snow, such an additional strength, as well as the reinforcement of such a strict watchfulness on the part of their servants having the care of the said reservoir, as may prevent any future

> breach or overflow of the said waters of the reservoir which they are of opinion has not, on the late occasion, been sufficiently attended to.'

It was not the 'main head' which had given way but the auxiliary head (or 'waste weir') from which water fell to the river below, and the necessary repairs were effected within a few weeks. To improve the supervision it was decided to install a supervisor in a cottage at the north (Kingsbury) end of the dam and near the end of 1841 this was done. When all the work was completed the canal company's management committee made an inspection, after which they held a committee meeting in Reservoir cottage. By 1851 a more assured water supply was needed from the reservoir and Parliament authorised its enlargement at a cost of £25,000.

Adjoining the south bank of the river, between the road to Kingsbury and the reservoir, lay Reservoir farm, occupied by George Field, whose son George was still there thirty years later. South and east of this farm, the 'hospital' land had gained 2½ acres under the Enclosure Award of 1823 but later lost 10 acres as a result of the building of the reservoir in about 1835 and subsequently another 9 acres, mainly because of the 1851–53 enlargement. After the long tenancy of the Nicolls from about 1730 and Ibberson's 20-year occupation after 1773 there was a string of short-term tenants including William Challoner, James Ackland and Job Roberts before things became more stable with 14-year tenancies by John Philpott (1814–29) and James Thompson (1829–43). In 1851 the land had just acquired some small timber-built farm buildings but still no house. The meadows near the river were said to be wet but generally the land had good hay crops and was much used for the grazing of horses.

On the other side of the road the hospital had some detached bits of land and the Finch family still owned the stretch of land they had bought in 1780. In 1851 Willesden parish still had a pound and a pond at Neasdon but these were sold to Joseph Nicoll in the following year for £50.

According to the 1851 census Neasdon contained fewer than a hundred souls on the night of Sunday 30th March. This is almost certainly too low a figure for the normal number of inhabitants. Both George Dean, a coachman, and Joseph Cook, a groom, were absent on census night from their cottages near the forge, while Neasdon House seems to be missing entirely from the house count as well as from the count of population. But even though 110 would be a better figure for Neasdon in 1851 than 95, an upper crust of one senior moneyer at the Mint, three Lincoln's Inn attorneys and one stockbroker was a pretty rich one for a hamlet of its size.

E: The Will of Joseph Nicoll

In the autumn of 1851 Joseph Nicoll sat down to write his will. It had been a disturbed year. His income from the Mint had been cut to about a third of what it had previously been; and the trouble over the pew was still in the forefront of his mind, as is shown by the fact that three of the first eight lines of his will are concerned with it.

One major question was the future of Neasdon House and the Neasdon estate. It is quite likely that Joseph had made up his mind about this a few years earlier. His father had died in 1823, his only sister in 1824 and his mother in 1830. He was a bachelor himself, as were his two brothers. John (b. 1795) lived at Willesden Green. Thomas (b. 1798) had been a brewer at the Old Boar's Head in Gray's Inn lane (which seems to have belonged to Joseph) but recently he had moved to Borehamwood. With little prospect of having nephews to carry on his name at Neasdon, Joseph had to look further afield and his thoughts turned to his cousins at Copt hall Hendon. Joseph's senior uncle on his father's side had been Thomas Nicoll, the lieutenant-colonel, whose second son William had undoubtedly been Joseph's original choice as his successor at Neasdon House. But William died at Neasdon, married but childless, as we have seen, in 1839. William's elder brother Thomas now owned Copt hall, where he resided with his wife Emma Mary and their two-year-old daughter Mary Nicoll Nicoll; and his younger brother John was dead.

The lieutenant-colonel's fourth and last child Catherine Maria Nicoll (b. 1819) got her first name from her mother Catherine Clarke Lewis, the daughter of William Lewis. Born in Jamaica but educated in England, Lewis as first practised accountancy but later became a distiller with a share in the distilling firm of Christian & Lewis in High Holborn and was for many years secretary of the association of rectifying distillers. He was also a keen botanist, becoming in 1797 a fellow of the Linnean society of London and in 1802 one of the fifteen members of the first council of the society listed in its Royal Charter. In time he became disenchanted with the distillery trade and after the marriage of his daughter Catherine to Thomas Nicoll, the Hendon widower, in St Giles's Holborn in 1808 he lost no time, being himself a widower, in moving to Hendon to be near her. In his later years he became friendly with a young physician, William Prout, who advised him about his gout and other ailments.

The name Prout is uncommon outside the west country. William came from a branch of the family which had owned land in Gloucestershire for generations. Born in 1785, he first applied himself to physics where he is still remembered for Prout's 'law' or 'hypothesis' concerning atomic weights; but he switched in his twenties to medicine and studied for M.D. at Edinburgh from 1808 to 1811. There he met Agnes Adam, daughter of Dr Alexander Adam, an academic renowned for a treatise on Roman antiquities. After Prout had completed his medical education at Guy's and St Thomas's hospitals, he married Agnes in St John's church, Westminster, in 1814. Their first child, Hannah Mary, was born in 1815 in Bloomsbury but died three months later. Then came a son, John William, in 1816 and three more sons: Alexander Adam (named after his maternal grandfather) in 1818, Walter Robert in 1820 and Thomas Jones, born in Edinburgh in 1823. The Prouts had moved house to 40 Sackville street, on the north side of Piccadilly, before Elizabeth was born in 1826 and Agnes, their last child, in 1828.

In 1834 John Prout went up to Wadham college, Oxford, as a commoner (there were few scholarships in those days) and got a third class in *litterae humaniores* in 1838, proceeding to B.A. in 1839 and M.A. in 1841. At Wadham he met two brothers: Nathaniel Stainton, who was two years his senior, and John Stainton, his junior by three years. John Prout was called to the bar at Lincoln's Inn in 1841, having been admitted in 1837, and Nathaniel Stainton followed him there two years later. Nathaniel much later married John's sister Agnes while John married a girl called

Elizabeth (?Preston) who died in 1844 and was the first to be buried in the Prouts' family grave in Kensal Green cemetery.

It seems likely that it was not Nathaniel Stainton so much as an older barrister, William Stone Lewis, son of Dr Prout's friend William Lewis, who had the decisive influence on John Prout's choice of profession. W.S. Lewis was certainly friendly with John and it was his niece, Catherine Maria Nicoll, whom the widower John Prout married as his second wife in January 1847 at St James's church in Piccadilly. The bride's address was noted in the register as 40 Sackville street, where the Prout family had lived for over twenty years, while the bridegroom's was entered as the Royal College, Chelsea.[19] The two witnesses to the marriage were both from the bridegroom's side - Elizabeth his sister and Agnes his mother. The fact that Elizabeth signed first could indicate that she was especially close to her brother and sister-in-law; certainly there was to be a very strong, life-long attachment between the daughter of the marriage and her aunt Elizabeth.

The newlyweds set up house at 2 Ovington square, just off the Brompton road, and a baby daughter was born to them on 4th March 1848. Unhappily the mother died about a week after the birth at the age of 29. So it was a motherless little girl who on 15th April 1848 in St James's church was given her mother's name Catherine, her mother's maiden name Nicoll and her grandmother's maiden name Lewis; and Joseph Nicoll of Neasdon - her mother's cousin - stood as her godfather.

In November 1851 Joseph made his will leaving his Neasdon estate in trust for the infant Catherine Nicoll Lewis Prout, confident that the principal trustee John William Prout, a barrister from a landowning family, would manage things well. As we have seen, Joseph was not always careful in what he said. He had made an exaggerated claim in his evidence to the consistory court earlier in the year and now in his will he made two small mistakes. It was not important that he described young Catherine as being 4 years old when she was only 3 (she was in fact 'rising 4'). But his statement that she was his 'cousin' has been a trap for the unwary historian ever since; in fact she was his cousin's daughter or his 'cousin once removed'.

Joseph's will remained unchanged, apart from an unimportant addition in a later codicil, until his death at Neasdon House on Friday 11th February 1853. The list of 18 deaths published in *The Times* on the following Monday included the entry:

> 'On the 11th inst. at his residence Neasdon House Willesden Joseph Nicoll Esq, late senior moneyer at the Royal Mint, aged 64.'

On the next Friday Joseph's body was laid to rest in the family vault in the churchyard of St Mary's, Willesden. He had asked in his will to be buried there 'without pomp or ostentation'. But an eye-witness with a long memory was to remember the day as one of

> 'general mourning in Neasdon and old Willesden. The funeral was an imposing sight and was attended by all the local farmers in long black coats. The mourning coach was drawn by six horses wearing massive plumes and there were other trappings of a like character.'[20]

So the last bearer of the Nicoll surname disappeared from Neasdon some 135 years after the arrival of the first. It was unfortunate for the family's later reputation that

Joseph was a much less popular figure than his predecessors. He may well have been a difficult man to deal with, possibly because of the chronic paralysis from which he suffered, but he faithfully fulfilled his obligations in regard to the Neasdon House coal charity. Even here there were later to be complaints that he had made people fetch their coal from Neasdon House instead of arranging for it to be delivered to their houses – complaints which overlooked the simple fact that had deliveries been made by Joseph the delivery cost would have been a prior charge on the charity, as was the system later.* It was almost inevitable, given the trouble over the pew, that Joseph's name would not be remembered with affection and that this would permanently obscure the good work done by his family for the parish of Willesden for more than a century.

Joseph's personality does not emerge clearly from history. He is known to have bid nearly 300 guineas, unsuccessfully, for the famous 'Chandos' portrait of Shakespeare formerly owned by the Nicolls of Southgate when it was sold by the Duke of Buckingham-and-Chandos along with other contents of Stowe House in 1848;[21] but this probably represented a wish to recover a family heirloom rather than an aesthetic interest in pictures. A portrait of a man on horseback, with his groom, is said to be of Joseph Nicoll but active horsemanship was ruled out by his paralysis; and the fact that he had an apartment at the Mint as early as 1815 (normally only senior moneyers had such apartments) could indicate that he had this affliction from quite an early age.

**see Appendix III, c*

PART THREE
The Prout Era (1853-81)

A. Settling In

THE TWO TRUSTEES nominated in Joseph Nicoll's will to look after the infant Catherine's estate during her minority were John William Prout, her father, and Charles Tubbs of Worthing, a member of the Tubbs family who owned land next to Joseph's at Harlesden. A few days before the will was proved, Tubbs declined the role of trustee and Walter Adam, Catherine's great-uncle, who lived with the Prouts in Sackville street, took on the job in his place. The Tubbs family, however, does not entirely vanish from the story at this point: two years later Charles Tubbs's only daughter Lucy married John Prout's brother Walter, who was a major with the East India Company's forces and died of sunstroke at the siege of Cawnpore in the Mutiny of 1857.

In the spring of 1853 a case was heard in the court of Chancery which resulted in the sum allowed out of the estate for Catherine's education and maintenance being raised to £1,500 a year and in John Prout being allowed to occupy Neasdon House. So Neasdon, in addition to its three Lincoln's Inn attorneys (the Hall brothers and W.W. Burton), now gained a barrister also belonging to Lincoln's Inn. It is not clear how active Prout was in the law at this time; though he had a business address in Lincoln's Inn Fields and subsequently in Carey street, his chief concern may well have been estate management at Neasdon. In 1856 he bought from the Hall brothers the Grove and Rose cottage. The Grove at this time was described as

> 'a detached family residence with extensive stabling, coachhouses and other offices, lawn, pleasure and kitchen gardens and about 37 acres of parklike meadow lands'.

Among its other features were

> 'fitted bookcases and glasses, lavatories, bath, coppers, piping and other fitted furniture, with a clock in the stable yard'.

Rose cottage, with gardens and outbuildings 'screened from the road by plantations and shrubbery and enclosed by wood palings' was occupied by William Marshall the stockbroker, on a lease running to 1858 or 1860 at the option of the tenant.

A plan included in the deed recording Prout's purchase of the Grove shows an unnamed farmhouse and farmbuildings lying on the south side of Dog lane, opposite

The GROVE*: plan of the property in 1856 when purchased by J. W. Prout, lessee of the Model Farm (on the left)*

the 'Dog' public house, on land said to be owned by All Souls College and leased to Prout. Prout seems to have had Elgar Prebble as his tenant and to have owned the farm ('The Model Farm') from a date which is uncertain.[22]

Prout also maintained Joseph Nicoll's strong line regarding Neasdon pews in the church. When he bought the Grove it was claimed in this transaction, as in the earlier one in 1817, that there were two pews in St Mary's appurtenant thereto. Apparently aware of the weakness of his claim to the Grove pews, Prout wrote to the church offering a compromise under which, at the end of a lease he had just offered to a tenant (presumably Mrs Charlotte Bigge), the pews would be converted into free sittings. The church's view, supported by the legal opinion of 1843, was that Prout had no rights in the matter and he may well have got no reply. The impasse over the Neasdon House pew was to continue throughout the 1860s and beyond.

Meanwhile at Neasdon House young Catherine was growing up under the care of grannie Agnes and aunt Elizabeth. Her uncle Thomas Jones Prout, after taking a moderate degree at Christ Church, Oxford, entered holy orders in 1849 and became a tutor of the college two years later. He used to visit his relations at Neasdon House during the vacations and soon after the Prouts' first Xmas at Neasdon he preached in St Mary's one Sunday at both morning and afternoon service. Another guest that first Xmas would have been another unmarried brother Alexander Adam Prout (MRCS) who now lived at the Royal Hospital, Chelsea, where he had held the post of assistant surgeon since 1846, and who was to die at Neasdon House in September 1854, presumably during a summer visit. Nine years later in 1863 grannie Agnes too died at Neasdon House aged 70 and was buried in the same grave as her husband William, her daughter-in-law Elizabeth and her son Alexander Adam. In that same year 1863 plans were deposited which were to bring the first railway to Neasdon.

B: Neasdon's First Railway

The hamlet of Neasdon acquired its first railway not because a London company was reaching out through the villages of Middlesex towards the industrial midlands but because a local company in the midlands was planning to build its own line down to the metropolis.

In the early 1840s the Midland Counties (later 'Midland') railway, based in Derby, extended no further south than Rugby on the line from Birmingham to Euston. In 1857 a new stretch of line was opened branching from the existing Midland line about 5 miles south of Leicester and running some 45 miles to Bedford, whence an extension line ran to Hitchin, a station on the Great Northern's line to King's Cross. But the Midland wanted its own track to London and in 1863 Parliament approved plans for a 50-mile line from Bedford to a new terminus in the Euston road in the parish of St Pancras.

Railway companies constructing lines between London and the towns of the midlands and the north-west had to find a way past the topographical obstacles of Middlesex, the chief of which was the heights of Hampstead. Robert Stephenson had chosen to keep his London-Birmingham line to the south of the long Brondesbury ridge and to make for the low ground south of Harlesden, approaching quite close to the Grand Junction canal at Lower place before swinging north through Wembley. The Midland company, approaching from the north, decided to follow the line of the ancient Edgware road between West Hendon and West Hampstead, through the gap at the eastern end of the Dollis hill ridge, and to slice through the Brondesbury ridge with a deep cutting east of Shoot-up hill.

Almost immediately, further plans were laid for a 7-mile line from Finchley, on the Edgware-Highgate-London line, to Acton, west of London; it would cross the new main line near Cricklewood, where two curves would connect both Finchley and Acton with Hendon to the north. However, by the time legislation was ready in 1864, these plans had been drastically curtailed: there was to be nothing east of the new main line, leaving only a 4¼-mile track linking Hendon and Acton.

As soon as plans for a Finchley Willesden and Acton railway became known late in 1863 the Willesden Vestry went into action, setting up a committee to protect the interests of the parish. The committee successfully negotiated eight clauses for inclusion in the bill 'for the protection of the Vicar and Inhabitants of the Parish of

The Two Ridges of Willesden

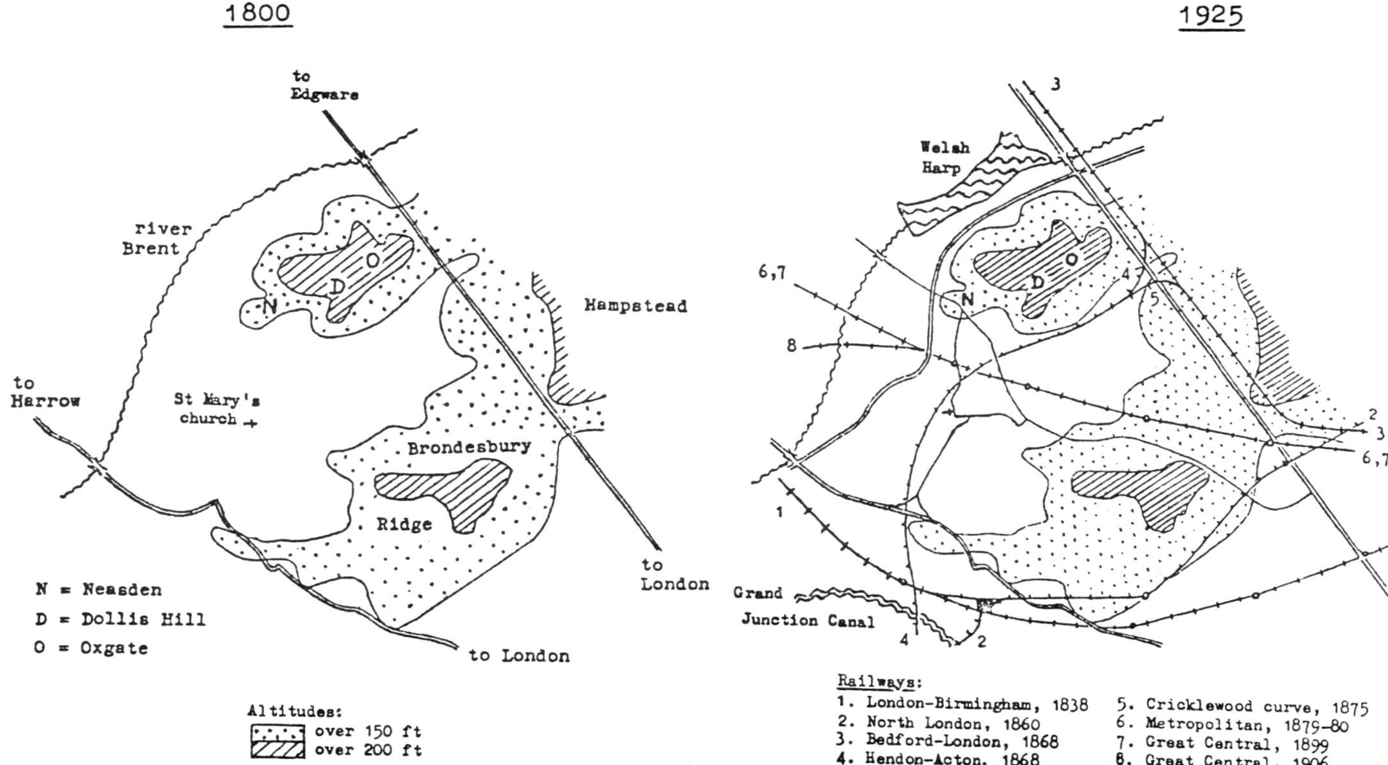

The proposed Finchley Willesden & Acton railway:

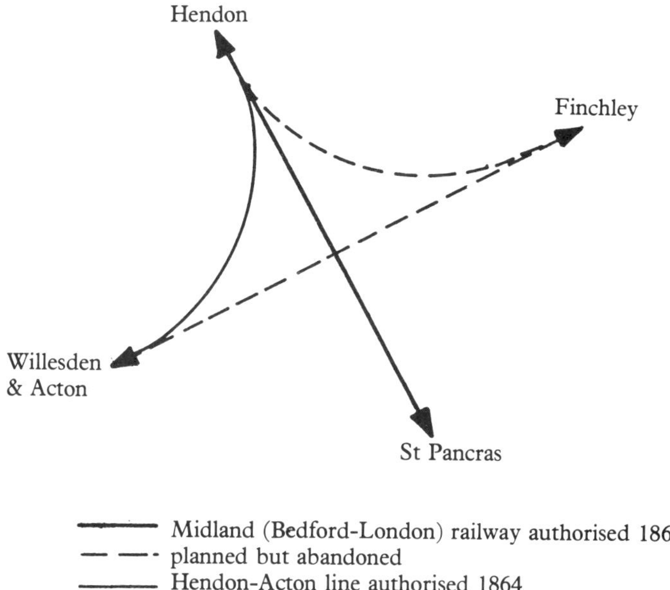

Willesden', of which five concerned the siting of the railway in relation to Neasdon lane and the parish church. The railway had to be kept at least 170 yards from the church and no train could come within 200 yards of Neasdon lane during morning service on Sundays, on Christmas Day or on Good Friday. On the subject of a passenger station within the parish:

> 'A station... shall be constructed... between [Neasdon lane] and a point half a mile from thence towards the Edgware road; and if there shall be 4, or less than 4, passenger trains each way daily, in the first case at least 4 of the passenger trains, and in the second case all of the passenger trains, shall stop daily (Sundays, Christmas Days and Good Fridays excepted) at the said station for the setting down and taking up of passengers, but the station shall not be made at [Neasdon lane] or within two hundred yards thereof nor shall there be any approach to or from [Neasdon lane] without the consent of the Vicar for the time being and the Inhabitants of the said Parish in Vestry assembled'.

The natural inference to be drawn from these provisions, which later appeared as sub-section six of section forty-six of the Act, is that the parish did not want noisy, smoky locomotives stopping and starting and blowing off steam close to the church and Neasdon lane. It was quite usual for college dons and cathedral chapters to insist that the hissing, clanking monsters be kept well away from their peaceful cloisters, even though they might later think differently; and it was a real worry to everyone in an age of horse-drawn transport that noisy locomotives near to highways frequently caused horses on the road to bolt, sometimes with disastrous results.

In March 1864 the committee reported back to the Vestry on the outcome of the negotiations, but the minutes make no mention of the restrictions to be placed on the siting of the station east of Neasdon lane. The requirements of the Act were in the event met by building a station just to the east of Dudding hill lane which was in existence by 1871. It was first used for passengers in August 1875, but by then Church End folk had already realised, too late, that the station had been built in quite the wrong place for their convenience.

Among the landowners required to cede land to the new railway were the Prouts of Neasdon, who received £2,279 for lands west of Dudding hill. The railway also took part of the two-acre parish close at Harlesden which was used as allotment gardens. The rents paid by the allotment holders had been a minor source of income for the Willesden charities and the capital sum of £837.14.0 received from the railway for not much more than half an acre of ground now became one of their major assets.

The Hendon-Acton line, built between 1864 and 1868 by a specially formed company called the Midland and South-Western junction railway, in which the Midland had a one-third interest, was opened for goods traffic on the same day (1st October 1868) that the main Bedford-St Pancras line with its majestic terminus came into full operation. It passed along the north-west face of Dudding hill and soon became known as the 'Dudding hill loop'. It then crossed the low ground near Neasdon lane by embankment and bridge until further to the south-west it met rising ground, passing under both the old and new Harrow roads at Craven park and over the London & North Western at Harlesden.

The 1864 Act had provided for a passenger service on the line with specified maximum fares.* For a journey of over two miles the maximum fare for a first-class passenger was to be 3d a mile with a luggage allowance of 120 lb, 2d a mile for a second class (luggage allowance 100 lb) and 1¼d a mile for third class (luggage allowance 60 lb). Maximum freight rates were also prescribed for various classes of merchandise, including livestock, and for the transport of carriages. In the event, a passenger service was not introduced on the line until the Midland, which had operated the railway from the start and was empowered to absorb it by an Act of 1867, had got permission in an Act of 1871 to add a curve about ¾-mile long branching off from the original line about ½-mile west of the Edgware road and swinging in a gentle curve over the road to join the main Midland line at Child's hill (Cricklewood) station; and it was four more years before construction was completed.*

At last in August 1875 all was ready for the inauguration of a passenger service on a sort of ring railway linking Moorgate, St Pancras and Cricklewood with Harlesden, Acton and Richmond. The station near Neasdon required by the 1864 Act was sited about one hundred yards east of Dudding hill lane and was later advertised as 'Dudding hill, for Willesden and Neasden'. The main exit from the station was on the south side of the line, whence a road on the line of the later Aberdeen road led to the summit of the hill and the main road. From Dudding hill station trains took four minutes to reach Harrow-road station and five minutes to get to Child's hill. On weekdays they ran at approximately hourly intervals up to 10 a.m. and similarly in the early evening, but less frequently at other times; and after the first year there were no trains on Sundays.

**see Appendix VII*

Now, for the first time, Neasdon folk had public transport available close at hand for journeys into London and further afield. People with business in the city, who had previously taken the 8.30 a.m. horse-bus from Church End, arriving back at 8.30 p.m. in the evening, now had a choice of trains and for regular commuters season tickets were on offer. But the railway company's heart was never really in the passenger service, which they ran because it was in the Act and they had to. Shortly after the service began one critic observed about the Dudding hill station:

> 'The approaches to the station defy description. From the Dudding hill road there are two:- one from the summit of the bridge, the descent from which is perilous in the extreme as it is so steep that passengers are obliged to run and frequently find themselves on the railway before they know where they are. The other approach is awkward and circuitous. As the winter comes on, persons in the Church End district will find it impossible to get at the railway by means of the Dudding hill footpath owing to so much wet clinging to the grass.'[23]

C: Willesden battles, North -v- South

The seven years which separated the start of freight services on the Acton branch line and the introduction of the passenger service were also those which saw momentous changes affecting the whole future of Willesden. From March 1868 people in Willesden were able to read about events, both in their own parish and in the larger world outside, in the weekly newpaper *The Kilburn Times.* The paper was edited and published in south Kilburn but covered the whole of Willesden parish, including Neasdon. Controversial issues could now be aired in public not only at periodic meetings of the parish Vestry, as before, but also in the columns of the weekly paper - and there were soon to be plenty of controversies in Willesden.

One such controversy concerned the parish church of St Mary's, where a committee of the congregation was set up in 1870 to examine current problems, including the growing problem of accommodation. In the twenty years since 1851 the population had grown from three to sixteen thousand, with no comparable increase in seating in the church. One way of solving the problem, indeed the obvious way, was to establish new churches in the various districts of Willesden. According to F.A. Wood, who was secretary of the church committee, John Prout of Neasdon House thought that people living within the new parish of Christ Church Brondesbury in Willesden lane should attend services there and not be catered for at St Mary's; and James Wright of Harlesden publicly offered an acre of his land for a new church there. Others took a different view, arguing that the parishioners of Willesden had the right to attend services in the old parish church, which should be enlarged to provide more seats, especially as Christ Church was in the nature of a 'proprietary' church, having been built with funds supplied by the family of Dr Williams, its first incumbent. In particular they denounced Prout's insistence on retaining the 'obnoxious' Neasdon House pew in St Mary's which prevented a satisfactory arrangement of the seating in part of the nave. Prout had no fiercer critic in all this than F.A. Wood, who had the steady support of the Editor of the *Kilburn Times.*

In October 1871 a general meeting of the congregation of St Mary's was held to consider the committee's report about further enlargement of the church. The meeting agreed with the committee that a north aisle should be built (it turned out later that a north aisle had in fact existed at an earlier period). Extracts were read from letters from Prout saying that the outside door in the north side of the chancel which Neasdon people used should be retained but it was later decided that a door and porch should be built in the new north aisle 'for the convenience of parishioners living at Neasdon'.[24]

The necessary work was completed within a year and the church re-opened its doors in October 1872. But harmony was still not achieved. On the last Sunday of 1872, when the customary service was held for collecting alms for winter clothing for the poor, the Prout family were seen to leave the church by the new 'Neasdon door' during the offertory hymn, which was apparently an innovation replacing the tradition of collecting the alms at the church door at the close of the service. This act of protest by the Prouts elicited a detailed note in the next issue of the *Kilburn Times*, followed by lengthy letters from readers about lowering the height of the pew, which (it was claimed) would be a simple job for a carpenter. Nothing happened, however, except that when John Prout thereafter attended morning service he would leave before the start of the sermon, presumably as a demonstration of his dislike of the vicar and his ways.

But by this time a much weightier issue held the centre of the stage in Willesden. In 1835 a significant modification of the traditional system of parish-based local administration had occurred when under the Poor Law Amendment Act of the previous year the Poor Law Commissioners brigaded Willesden with seven other parishes to form the Hendon Union for poor law administration. In fact the Union actually operated from Edgware, not Hendon, and when an analogous body was set up with responsibility for highways in the same eight parishes in 1863 it was called the Edgware Highways District Board. The populations of these parishes in 1831, 1851 and 1871 were, according to the Union's own statistics:-

Parish	*Numbers*			*Percentages*		
	1831	1851	1871	1831	1851	1871
Harrow	3,861	4,951	8,545	29	31	23
Hendon	3,110	3,333	6,955	23	21	19
Pinner	1,270	1,310	2,322	10	8	6
Great Stanmore	1,144	1,180	1,355	9	7	4
Little Stanmore	876	811	816	7	5	2
Edgware	591	765	655	4	5	2
Kingsbury	463	606	621	4	4	2
WILLESDEN	1,876	2,961	15,866	14	19	43
Total	13,191	15,917	37,135	100	100	100*

**does not add because of rounding*

Clearly by 1871 Willesden was no longer a wholly agricultural parish but it was not wholly urban either. London's expanding population had flowed into the southern part of the parish, encouraged by the growth of transport facilities, and although this urbanised area was reckoned to account for only ten per cent of the four thousand acres of ground which made up the parish it contained the majority of its inhabitants.

The environmental needs of the urbanised area in the south were naturally very different from those of the agricultural area in the north. In addition the Brondesbury ridge formed a watershed right across the parish. The area south of the watershed drained naturally through the metropolis to the Thames but from the larger agricultural area north of it, including Cricklewood and Willesden Green, drainage was into the river Brent, either directly from the north face of the Dollis hill ridge or by way of the Slade brook ('Neasdon valley') running between the two ridges and reaching the Brent at Stonebridge. So when the question of local public health organisation, including drainage and sanitation, came to the fore in Willesden in the early 1870s it is not surprising that sharply different views about what was needed were taken by the urbanised population of the Kilburn area on the one side and the farming people of the agricultural north on the other.

Concern about public health in England was active and vocal in the early years of Queen Victoria's reign, resulting in the Public Health Act of 1848 which set up a central health board in London and allowed for the creation of local health boards at the wish of local communities. This was followed by the Local Government Act of 1858 which provided for the establishment of local boards for the general administration of local affairs and in 1871 a central Local Government Board was created with its office in Downing street. Soon afterwards James Stansted, M.P., president of the Poor Law Board, introduced another public health bill which proposed to place responsibility for public health, including drainage and sanitation, in the same hands as responsibility for poor-law matters. It was this bill which alarmed the southern part of Willesden and spurred it into action.

Although Willesden in 1871 had 43 per cent of the Hendon Union's inhabitants, having quadrupled its population since 1861, it still had only four seats on the Union board of guardians and was therefore badly under-represented. The leaders of southern opinion, including the editor of the *Kilburn Times*, were convinced that if control of their drainage and sanitation were given to a body sitting six miles away in the rural surroundings of Edgware their urban needs would not properly be considered. To avert this disaster they proposed taking steps to get the 1858 Local Government Act 'adopted' by the parish of Willesden so that, if the Local Government Board agreed, responsibility for public health and highways would rest in future with a Willesden local board.

The 'Kilburnites' and their supporters were often referred to as the 'promoters' of the Act. The 'opponents' of the Act, including landowners like John Prout and the farmers in the agricultural north, argued that responsibility for drainage and sanitation in the Brent basin should rest with a single authority covering several parishes, so that a comprehensive solution could be worked out for the whole water area. If they could successfully oppose adoption of the Act, drainage and sanitation would automatically become the responsibility of the eight-parish Hendon Union when the 1872 public health bill became law; and this would suit them very well.

The 'promoters' now lost no time in getting a meeting called, as provided for in the

1858 Act, to debate the issue. Having failed to complete all its business on 16th July 1872, the meeting was adjourned to a day a fortnight later, when there was a large majority in favour. The 'opponents' immediately demanded a poll, as allowed by the Act, and this produced 441 votes for adoption and 343 against. Although the total number of votes cast was 784, the number of people voting was in fact smaller because each voter had a block of votes scaled to the amount of property he owned in Willesden, plus the amount of property he rented, and a large owner-occupier could dispose of as many as twelve votes.*

The 'opponents' seemed to have lost; but in fact they had a winning card up their sleeve. They pointed out to the Local Government Board in Whitehall that because the public meeting had been adjourned for a fortnight, instead of 'from day to day' as specified in the Act, its decisions and the results which flowed therefrom, including the poll, were invalid; and the Board agreed with this view. The 'promoters' complained vehemently in the *Kilburn Times* that their opponents had proposed the fourteen-day adjournment as a trick to invalidate the subsequent proceedings. The 'opponents' were jubilant and at a further meeting carried a motion forbidding further discussion of the issue for another twelve months. The 'promoters' would have none of this and got a meeting called in April 1873 at which they surprisingly lost the vote by about 4 to 1. Nothing daunted, they called for a poll which was duly taken in May 1873 and resulted in a win by a whisker for the promoters, the votes being:-

For the Act	678 votes	=	50.2%
Against the Act	673 votes	=	49.8%
Majority in favour	5 votes	=	0.4%

Predictably the opponents protested to the Local Government Board that the poll had not been taken in accordance with the provisions of the Act and in any case the majority in favour was too slender to be accepted as a basis for such an important decision as setting up a Willesden local board. Petitions against adoption of the Act were submitted by George Furness of Roundwood, John Peacock of Willesden Green and the Prouts of Neasdon. The Prout petition, signed by John Prout, his daughter Catherine (now aged twenty five), George Alderson (a Neasdon farmer) and four hundred and seventy two others, could well have represented practically the whole of the opposition vote in the poll, given the system of plural voting, but the list of names has not survived. They argued first that the poll was invalidated by irregularities and secondly that the Local Government Board's consent should be withheld until an on-the-spot inquiry had been held to gauge the feelings of the inhabitants and to assess the merits of the case for adoption and against.

The upshot was that in January 1874 a Board inspector held a seven-day official inquiry at the Vestry hall, Church End, followed by a personal tour round the parish. In his report he concluded that any irregularities in conducting the poll had not been serious and that on balance consent should be given to adoption of the Act for Willesden. Accordingly, a provisional Order was made by the Secretary of State in June 1874 saying that, on the Michaelmas day following the confirmatory Act of Parliament, Willesden would become an urban sanitary district and a local government

**see Appendix VI*

district subject to the jurisdiction of a local board; and this was confirmed a few weeks later in the Local Government Board's Provisional Order Confirmation Act 1874 (no. 4) on 30th July 1874.

In the event the Willesden Local Board came into operation a year later than intended, presumably because there was not enough time to settle the administrative details. In December 1874 it was decided to have four wards within the WLB area called South Kilburn, North Kilburn, East Willesden and West Willesden, electing respectively six, three, three and three members to a board of fifteen. Not for the last time in its history Neasdon was now split right down the middle, since the boundary between East and West Willesden was to be 'Kingsbury lane' (the road from Neasdon to Kingsbury bridge) and 'Dudding-hill lane'. In the south, East Willesden stretched down to the North London railway's Brondesbury station in Edgware road while West Willesden took in part of Harlesden. So the wards did not follow the natural hydrological boundary along the Brondesbury ridge; and the Kilburn wards had a built-in majority on the board. This was to cause trouble later.

The stage was now set for the first elections for the Willesden Local Board but even these were not without controversy. The nominees for East Willesden's three seats included Henry Baker, founder of a family firm of auctioneers, and his son Alfred, who acted as land agents for John Prout among others. The *Kilburn Times* now presumed to warn the electorate that anyone who was an agent of Prout would be merely his mouthpiece in the discussions of the local board. This was hardly fair comment considering the esteem in which Henry Baker, a man of over 60, was held in Willesden (Alfred was later the highly respected occupier of Harlesden lodge and a prominent member of the Pattenmakers Company in the City). The explanation is doubtless that the *Kilburn Times* was regularly the sounding-board for the views of F.A. Wood, who had recently had a public altercation with the Bakers in the newspaper over the sewerage arrangements for new houses in Nicoll road Harlesden. But the episode illustrates vividly the deep hostility which existed between the north and south of Willesden and which was to persist throughout the twenty years of the local board's existence and beyond.

As it happened, it was discovered that Alfred Baker lacked the property qualifications needed for candidature but Henry Baker, in spite of the *Kilburn Times*, came second to James Jackson in East Willesden. F.A. Wood, one of the successful candidates in South Kilburn, wanted Kershaw (who topped the poll in North Kilburn) to be made chairman of the new Board but the appointment went instead to George Furness of West Willesden. So the Board was headed, for the next six years, by one of the main opponents of its creation.

D: *Catherine Prout*

At Neasdon House Catherine Prout attained her majority in 1869 having been brought up largely by her grandmother and her aunt Elizabeth. She was probably educated at home but no governess was enumerated there on census night 1861, although the 1871 census contains an entry for a French governess born in Prussia.

Catherine marked her coming of age by giving the parish a large clock for the church tower. In 1876, when one of its weights weighing about three cwt crashed into the baptistry beneath, fortunately missing the valuable font, the *Kilburn Times* reckoned that the clock had originally cost about £300, adding the sour comment that 'ever since, it has been a source of considerable expense to the church who have to keep it in repair'. But the clock was a sturdy one and was to outlast all its critics: on 4th March 1969 a commemorative ring on the church bells marked its centenary.

From about 1860 onwards the Prouts gave each year a summer treat to the schoolchildren of Willesden in the grounds of Neasdon House. In 1873 a newspaper report spoke of games and tea on the lawn on a fine day in mid-July, going on until 8 o'clock in the evening. The report added coyly that this would be the last treat Miss Prout would give under that name because in a few months' time she was to become 'somebody else'. Her affiancé, as announced in the newspaper two months earlier, was William Edward Nicol from far-away Aberdeenshire.

About twenty miles east of Balmoral and thirty miles from the coast at Aberdeen, the town of Aboyne stands on the bank of the river Dee, overlooked from the south-east by the estates of Ballogie and Midstrath and the hill of Balnacraig. Here, covering 7,000 acres, lay the lands of James Dyce Nicol, who lived partly at Ballogie and partly, since becoming M.P. for Kincardineshire in 1865, in Bayswater, London. In London in 1866 he was sponsored for a fellowship in the prestigious Royal Geographical Society by Sir Robert Murchison, the eminent geologist. Nicol's eldest son and heir William, born in 1846, received a business training in London and must have spent long periods at his parents' London house in Hyde park terrace, as he did later after his father's death in November 1872.

Another fellow of the R.G.S. at this time was John William Prout, who had been sponsored for his fellowship in 1852, when he was living in Lincoln's Inn Fields, by Robert Brown the distinguished botanist. It is not clear how John Prout knew Brown but, before he became keeper of the botanical collections in the British Museum, Brown was from 1805 to 1822 librarian of the Linnaean Society and would certainly have known there William Lewis, grandfather of Prout's wife, and possibly also Prout's father, the famous physician, who was Lewis's close friend.

At the R.G.S. monthly meetings John Prout would undoubtedly have talked to J.D. Nicol and it is possible that his daughter Catherine first met young William Nicol at one of the society's social gatherings ('conversaziones'). However that may have been, it became known in May 1873 that a marriage would take place later that year. The young pair seem to have had much in common. Both were substantial landowners; both were extrovert in character. William was bluff, hearty and genial by nature, vigorous and enthusiastic; Catherine, known in the family as Kitty, was a lively person and a strong personality.

A lengthy marriage settlement compiled no doubt by John Prout, who was now practising in the Court of Equity, was signed and sealed two days before the wedding day, Thursday, 20th November 1873. Much of the Wednesday afternoon seems to have been spent putting up flags and bunting on the roads between Neasdon House and the church and between the church and the Willesden Green 'Spotted Dog', where a large triumphal arch spanned the road. The following morning, as befitted a parish holiday, dawned fine and sunny. No expense had been spared on the arrangements and the church was filled to overflowing. The bride was attended by six bridesmaids, including her cousin Mary Nicoll Nicoll from Copt hall, Hendon, and the knot was tied by Catherine's uncle the Rev. Thomas Jones Prout, who had come over from Oxford.[25] After the ceremony the line of carriages taking the guests up the hill to a 'recherché déjeuner' at Neasdon House formed an almost continuous procession along the mile-long route. In the evening coloured lights outside Neasdon's 'Spotted Dog' showed 'P' and 'N' linked together. There were similar festivities on the Scottish estates on Deeside lasting until three o'clock in the morning and two lengthy epithalamic odes appeared in the Aberdeen newspaper.

E: Advance of the Metropolitan

As Catherine Prout's wedding procession made its way in November 1873 past the 'Spotted Dog' and towards the church it had to pass under the bridge carrying the Acton branch railway line over Neasdon lane. A generation earlier the famous headmaster Thomas Arnold, standing on an arch of the Euston-Birmingham line at Rugby, had rejoiced that the railways, though unsightly, were liberating England from feudalism.[26] People watching in Neasdon lane in 1873 might well have wondered how long the considerable elements of feudality which still persisted in the neighbourhood could last before the old social framework fell apart. The Acton branch line was the first of Neasdon's railways but already in the summer of 1873 Parliament had authorised the building of another railway which was to change the face of west Neasdon and to start in earnest Neasdon's development from a hamlet into a suburb.

In 1863 the first London underground trains started running on the Metropolitan line between Paddington and Farringdon street, stopping at the Baker Street station on the way; and from Baker Street in 1868 an extension line was projected to Swiss Cottage. Four years later in the autumn of 1872 the Metropolitan deposited plans for a further extension of the line to a terminus on the south-east bank of the Brent some 270 yards downstream from Kingsbury bridge. The railway was named the 'Extension to Kingsbury' although the end of the line was to be in a field in Neasdon Bottom which was a detached piece of 'the hospital land'.

Willesden people were not slow to understand what the company's plans meant, as a perceptive letter to the *Kilburn Times* in May 1873 (by F.A. Wood) clearly shows:

> 'The company propose to take more than 100 acres of land for the purpose of building workshops, engine sheds, labourers' cottages and all the erections necessary for a gigantic factory for the purpose of making, repairing and housing their extensive rolling stock. The ratepayers of that portion of the parish might be reconciled to the creation of a vast town of workshops if they could obtain easier access to London in the shape of convenient stations and trains running at suitable hours... It will create a town where there is now nothing but green fields; it will bring a large population to a place where there are not now half a dozen inhabitants. If the company will give facilities for direct access to London the value of the adjacent land will be enormously increased and the property will most probably be thickly built on.'

At the Edgware Highways District Board it was suggested

> 'that the company should be required to erect convenient stations and give a proper service of trains and that the board refuse to sanction the taking of land fronting the road from Neasdon to Kingsbury... the company should not be allowed to spoil the beauty of the neighbourhood.'

Such sentiments would have stood little chance of being heeded, had not most of the land which the company wanted to purchase belonged to the Prouts, who were prepared to fight. A petition was lodged against the bill in the names of John Prout and his daughter Catherine and the case was heard by a House of Lords committee in the spring of 1873, all the parties being represented by learned counsel. The outcome was an agreement between the Prouts and the railway company which was later referred to in section fifty-nine of the 1873 Act and printed in full in a schedule thereto.* After stating that John Prout had appeared before a committee of the House of Lords with his daughter Catherine, as a petitioner against the bill, the schedule listed nine heads of agreement including one requiring a station to be built at some point between the Acton branch line and the Kingsbury terminus; from this origin came, seven years later, the station at Neasdon lane.

But this was only the first part of the story. Four months after the passing of the Act, for reasons explained in Part Five below, further plans were deposited for building an extension of the Metropolitan to Harrow-on-the-hill.* The new line would diverge from the line to the Kingsbury terminus at a point 'about 200 yards south of Model Farm' (i.e. a little to the west of Neasdon lane) and head for the low ground at Wembley park. The company would be allowed to buy not only the land needed for the new line itself, with the usual allowance for 'deviation', but also the wedge of land lying between this new swathe of ground and what had been authorised in the 1873 Act. Again the Prouts petitioned, but most of the running was made this time by the London & North Western railway which contended that traffic on its line through Harrow Weald would be damaged by the new Metropolitan line to Harrow-on-the-hill and that the Metropolitan had undertaken during the passage of the 1873 Act not to continue this line beyond Kingsbury. The petition failed, but both the 1873 and 1874 petitions reflect the general tendency for railway bills to incur opposition from two main sources: the landowners, and rival transport interests such as canals and other railways.

Frequently landowners opposed railway bills not because they had any real hopes of preventing a railway being constructed but as a means of getting a higher price for their land. Acts of Parliament gave railway companies the right to acquire land but if the parties could not mutually agree terms the issue had to go to arbitration. It seems to have been customary for landowners to claim, and to be given, a price for their land which reflected its value to the purchaser's enterprise rather than its current-use value to the seller. At the 1873 hearing the Ecclesiastical Commissioners were said to be getting £300 an acre for land at Willesden Green. When negotiations started later between the Prouts and the Metropolitan, the railway offered £200 an acre while the Prouts asked for about £450. Eventually the arbitrator settled on a figure of £83,450 which almost exactly split the difference between the two claims.

**see Appendix VII*

About half of the total of 252 acres bought by the railway from the Prouts belonged to Newman's farm, which (as Neasdon Farm) had been for generations the largest farm in the hamlet. In October 1876 much of the livestock, mainly cattle and pigs, was sold off and subsequently the truncated farm specialised, like Model Farm nearby, in horses.

NEASDEN STATION: (above) 1896 – a 'Met' train starts on its non-stop run to Harrow

(left) 1970 – before the old superstructure was removed

With the land questions settled, the Metropolitan was able to push its tracks forward to Willesden Green in 1879 and to Neasden and Harrow in 1880. It was an indication of the openness of the country west of Neasden that no station was felt to be needed in the four miles and more between Neasden and Harrow until a stop was constructed at Wembley Park in 1894.

The line approached Neasden through a deep cutting along the southern slopes of Dudden hill, passing successively under Dudden hill lane, the Acton branch line and Neasden lane, which was carried over the tracks on an embankment about thirty yards west of its old path. The station at Neasden lane, officially named Kingsbury-and-Neasden though known popularly and even in railway literature as Neasden, was built in the style of a house above the tracks with staircases for the Up and Down platforms.[27] In August 1880 there were over thirty trains daily each way between Baker Street and Harrow completing the ten-mile run in half an hour. From Neasden to Baker Street the journey took twenty minutes with seven intermediate stops while the non-stop run to Harrow took only nine minutes. The second-class fare from Neasden to Baker Street was seven old pence (= three new pence approximately) – enough to buy in those days 4 lb of bread. A second-class quarterly season ticket over the same route cost thirty-two shillings (£1.60), plus five per cent Inland Revenue tax.

Neasden commuters could now get into London either by the Midland's Acton branch line from Dudding hill or by the Metropolitan line from Neasden lane. For Harlesden folk there was a similar choice between Willesden Junction, the Midland's Harrow road station and the Metropolitan at Neasden, to which a horse-bus ran from St Mary's road Harlesden (later the Royal Oak) via Church road. This bus service originated in an offer made in February 1880 by William Memory, who already ran a bus to Willesden Junction from Stonebridge park, to John Bell, general manager of the Metropolitan. It was always expected that the service would run at a loss but a moderate deficit could be justified if it attracted to the railway people who would not otherwise have travelled. Memory proved a difficult contractor and when the initial contract expired in March 1881 the follow-on contract was given to John Cakebread, another Harlesden man with livery stables in Avenue road. In 1882 the Neasden stationmaster reported to Bell that many people used the bus only on wet and muddy days, and the deficit mounted steadily. When the service was threatened with closure near the end of 1883 the vicar of Willesden was one who wrote to plead for its continuation, but the reprieve lasted less than two years and closure came in October 1885.

F: Prout's Neasdon

Ten months after the Metropolitan railway arrived and four months after old James Wright of Harlesden died in retirement at Brighton, John William Prout died at Neasdon House on 2nd June 1881 and was buried, as he had wished, 'in Brompton churchyard in the same grave with my beloved wife Catherine'. This was not in Brompton cemetery, as the *Willesden Chronicle* (founded 1877) reported, but in the churchyard of Holy Trinity Brompton, just across the Brompton road from Ovington square where Prout and his wife were living when their daughter Catherine was born in 1848.

In his 28 years at Neasdon House Prout had in general maintained the tradition he inherited from Joseph Nicoll. In particular he carried through a fourth wave of land acquisitions comparable to the earlier acquisitions of Thomas Nicoll the elder, John Nicoll (d. 1819) and Joseph (d. 1853), so that by 1875 the Prout family owned practically all the land at Neasdon.

As noted earlier, Prout bought the Grove and Rose cottage in 1856, when the Hall brothers had got into financial difficulties. Described as solicitors and farmers (or cattledealers) of Neasdon, they were stated in a bankruptcy court case in 1857 to have assets of under £13,000, mainly in the form of animals, while there were liabilities of over £100,000. Soon afterwards they left Neasdon and were succeeded at the Grove, as Prout's tenants, by Mrs Charlotte Bigge, Richard Wright the attorney from Harlesden, Captain Guiness and Thomas Hopkinson, a member of the well-known firm of piano-makers who outlived Prout by a few months. In 1874 the stockbroking Marshall family left Rose cottage (already for some time known as the Grange) after residing there continuously, apart from one short interval, for about thirty years; and Charles Rotherham, a dog vet, arrived a few years later. At the farm across the road the solicitor W.W. Burton left Neasdon some time in the 1850s.

In 1864 Prout bought from the dean and chapter of Westminster the land and house (later known as Neasdon cottage) which he already held on lease. The lease granted by the Abbey to Edmund Roberts in 1554 for 99 years had almost expired when the property was sold in 1651 to Sir William Roberts 'farmer of lands in Willesden'; but the ancient annual rent was one of the revenues for the maintenance of Westminster school and almshouses, and this was reserved during the Commonwealth period to the newly formed board of governors for the school and almshouses which for a time replaced the dean and chapter. Early in the 18th century, when ownership had reverted to the Abbey, William Hawkins vicar of Willesden was the lessee, followed later by his son William, his son's widow Lydia and then, until 1811, by Thomas Moore, who had married Lydia's great-niece. After a few years in the hands of James Hall, the lease was taken over in 1818 by John Nicoll of Neasdon House. Thereafter, though the leases were invariably for twenty-one years, it was customary for each lease to be renewed after seven years, the names of successive lessees being in 1825 Elizabeth Nicoll, widow of John, in 1832 1839 and 1846 Joseph Nicoll, in 1853 the co-trustees John Prout and Walter Adam, and in 1860 John Prout alone. From 1861 the tenant was James Wilson Pearl, a farmer and horsedealer.

For a time about 1860 a well-known surgeon of the Westminster Hospital, Barnard Wight Holt (born about 1817, FRCS 1847), had an address in Neasdon. It was said of him that he loved horses, was an excellent judge of them, rode regularly to hounds and had a carriage and pair among the best in London. When he retired from his post as senior surgeon and teacher at the hospital in 1873 he practised privately from premises in Savile Row but remained both a consultant at the hospital and for some years a member of its council. He also became proprietor of Newman's well-known livery stables in Regent street. It is not clear, however, whether Holt knew the Newmans, who occupied Neasdon Farm, before his time at Neasdon or because of it. Although his middle name Wight is the same as that of the Rev. Moses Wight, a former vicar of Willesden, there is no evidence of a connexion.

At the northern end of Neasdon Prout acquired the hospital land in a rather roundabout way. In February 1871, knowing that the fourteen-year lease held by Augustus Lines (a resident of St John's Wood) would be falling in ten months later, Prout had his solicitors write to the treasurer of Christ's hospital offering to buy all its bits of land at Willesden which lay detached from the main group of hospital fields bordering the Brent reservoir. Prout's motive in making this offer, at a price equivalent to 50 years' rent, was apparently to get hold of an acre of land owned by the hospital in Church road, near St Mary's, which was eminently suitable for building. The hospital promptly consulted the Wandsworth authorities who put the idea to the Charity Commissioners. Sensing an opportunity to sell off the entire Willesden estate on advantageous terms, they agreed to make Prout a counter-offer to sell him their whole estate for £9,200.

The hospital estate consisted at this time of 'forty-six acres of grassland, a very small mean cottage built in 1858 at a cost of £105, a range of timber-built tiled outbuildings built in 1848–49 and timber valued at £16'. The cottage, located beside the Neasdon-Kingsbury road, was 'brick-built with two rooms and pantry on the ground floor'; and a tool-house with a room over it completed, with the usual outbuildings, a serviceable but badly constructed ensemble. Prout's estate agents (the Bakers) thought the price very high, as did everyone else, but he eventually agreed and a draft agreement was drawn up. Nobody at the time knew of the Metropolitan's plans to take the detached part of the hospital land in Neasdon Bottom, nor did the Metropolitan's lawyers know of Prout's agreement with the hospital when they submitted the company's plans in November 1872. In November 1873 the price was adjusted slightly to £9,400, partly because of a small increase in the estimated area of the land. Notice of the intention to sell was duly affixed to the door of St Mary's church and advertised in *The Times* and elsewhere, and the sale was completed early in 1874.

We can only guess at Prout's motives in buying this land at a price 'very much beyond what an indifferent purchaser would pay'. If he bought it for its development potential, he and his heirs had in the event over half a century to wait before they could take their profit. The Wandsworth charities, on the other hand, did very well for themselves by selling; instead of a possible rent of £130 a year from a tenant-farmer, plus the potential value of the Church road building plot, they got an assured income of £300 a year by investing the proceeds in 3% Consols. So, after 170 years, the era of 'the hospital land' at Neasdon came to an end. The land was later farmed by William Burton, tenant of what remained of Neasdon Farm.

A few months before his death Prout made his final land acquisition at Neasdon when he bought the farm which lay between the former hospital land, the river and the road to Kingsbury and which had been tenanted for many years by two George Fields, father and son. The part of the farm which adjoined the river had for long been known as 'gravel pit field' but it was only recently that the whole thirty-eight acres had been styled Gravel Pit Farm. In contrast, Prout got rid of The Model Farm, where Francis Sutton was bailiff for many years, selling it to John Edwards of Euston road in 1880, at the same time as he sold 'Neasdon park' (the land between the future Prout grove and the railway) to Henry Booth Hohler of Fawkham manor in Kent; the explanation may be that parts of both of these properties were by then due to be taken over by the Metropolitan under an Act of 1880.

With regard to his position in the community, Prout defended unyieldingly his right to keep unchanged the Neasdon House pew in the church and Neasdon House continued to be regarded locally as the bastion and symbol of 'ancien régime' in Willesden, embodying a degree of autocracy and paternalism which the democrats in the south of the parish found intolerable and were determined to overthrow. Possibly influenced by his womenfolk and especially by Catherine as she grew up, Prout took a more kindly view of his responsibilites to the community than his predecessor Joseph Nicoll. In addition to maintaining the Neasdon House charities it was apparently his custom at Christmas to distribute several hundredweight of beef to people in the neighbourhood. After Catherine had left Neasdon to live as Mrs Nicol in Kensington, Prout continued the tradition of the annual treat for the schoolchildren of Willesden at Neasdon House which had started about 1860. Catherine and her husband would be there with others of the family, organising games and waiting on the children at tea on the lawn in the shade of the fine old trees. For some hundreds of children the annual treat at Neasdon House was one of the high spots of the year, especially after the Wrights of Harlesden gave up doing something similar.

For Neasdon folk generally life certainly became more varied during Prout's time. Anyone standing at Neasdon green one August evening in 1871 could have seen a balloon floating slowly down to earth near Willesden church. After landing safely the balloonist, who had come by air from Woolwich, refreshed himself at the 'White Hart', folded up his balloon and conveyed it in a cart to Willesden Junction, whence he travelled home by rail; in this adventure he was perhaps inspired by the feat of the French leader Gambetta, who had escaped from Paris by balloon in October 1870 over the heads of the besieging Prussians to carry on the Government from Tours.

A more permanent attraction was the racecourse established by William Perkins Warner on the north side of the Brent reservoir near the Edgware road. Racecourses had always had a bad name for attracting the riff-raff but doubtless the more adventurous of Neasdon's young people would have flocked to the races there, especially on holidays like Whit Monday. They could have got there by train from Dudding hill station, changing at Child's hill for the new Welsh Harp station, but it would probably have been quicker to walk. If they had gone by the west end of the Brent reservoir they might occasionally have seen the wall of overflow water falling forty feet over the 60-foot semicircular dam. Possibly the biggest crowd Warner ever got was not for any of his race meetings nor at one of his Whit-Monday firework displays but when the 'Upper Welsh Harp' public house was destroyed by fire in February 1874. The blaze was clearly visible from Neasdon and it is said that in the next two days half of Willesden went to see the charred ruins.

William Burton, a 'jobmaster' with headquarters in Marylebone high street, who now occupied the hospital land, used to enter horses regularly in the Kingsbury races and on the last day of the 1876 spring meeting one of his racers worth £1,000 fell in a steeplechase and had to be destroyed. But generally his horse business at Neasdon flourished and for several weeks early in 1875, when horse prices were still high after an enormous increase during the Franco-Prussian war, groups of Spaniards were reported to be on Burton's land trying to buy horses for the Spanish Government.

Doubtless there were in Neasdon the usual competitions in various agricultural skills such as ploughing and hedge-laying. One special event in June 1876 was a mowing match over an area of about a hundred and fifty square yards between George Alderson (one of Prout's tenant-farmers) and W. Hyde of Church End. After Alderson's skill with the scythe had proved much superior to his adversary's, a leg-of-mutton supper was served for the competitors and other guests by George Twyford in the ornamental gardens of Neasdon's 'Spotted Dog', with the loser footing the bill. It was only in the 1880s that cricket and football came to be organised on a big scale; before then casual matches could have taken place anywhere where a friendly farmer could spare a piece of meadow. It was a way of life which the arrival of the Metropolitan railway with its small town of artisans was to do much to change.

PART FOUR
The First Transformation

A. The New Parish

WITH the Metropolitan railway constructed and in operation, the stage was set for the first major piece of development in Neasden's history. On the north of the line new carriage shops were built to replace the old ones at the Farringdon street depot and a preliminary diagram (possibly illustrating the maximum which could be done rather than what was actually intended) sketched out an estate of some three hundred and fifty workers' houses in the form of a square grid bounded on the north-west by the canal feeder and on the north-east by the Neasden-Kingsbury road.

The estate actually built in 1882 consisted of a hundred and twelve houses. One street, backing up to the feeder and called A-street, consisted of sixty houses in six blocks, the two end houses of each block being rather larger than the others. Parallel to A-street was B-street, consisting of similar houses, but there were only forty of them in four blocks. Unlike most railway cottages of the period they had quite long gardens at the back, especially those backing up to the feeder. On the Neasden-Kingsbury road itself, between A-street and B-street, a row of ten shops was built with two storeys of living accommodation above the ground floor; this stretch of road was henceforth known to everyone, including the Post Office, as Kingsbury road.

The whole estate of a hundred cottages and ten house-shops, with another two semi-detached houses close to the works for the supervisory staff, was to have cost about £27,000 but on the lowlying ground the builders (Messrs C.D.Jones) had more trouble with the foundations than they expected and the actual cost turned out some £3,000 higher than the estimate; and dampness was to remain a persistent problem after the houses were built. In the process of constructing the estate considerable damage was done to the Neasden-Kingsbury road and the Metropolitan agreed to give the Willesden Local Board £300 for reinstating the road.

After the railway workers started moving in on Good Friday 1882 the churches quickly took the lead in developing the social life of the new community. A nonconformist Sunday school, begun in one of the cottages in April, expanded rapidly and was allowed by the Metropolitan to occupy the ground floor of one of their shops in Kingsbury road. By December 1882 the school contained nearly a hundred children, while a similar number of people regularly filled the same rooms on Sunday evenings for church services. The railway was able to continue this arrangement over a long period since rarely were more than six of the ten shops occupied at any one time. In addition the Metropolitan regularly contributed £10 a year towards the mission's running expenses.

Early in 1883 the Church of England's diocesan home mission appointed as their missionary to the new estate the Rev. James Mills, who was then curate of St Andrew's Kensington. The curacy was to be called St Saviour's and the Metropolitan generously gave a site at the corner of A-street beside the canal feeder for the construction of a mission building. In July 1883 Mills launched an appeal for money to finance the project with a subscription list headed by the owners and tenants of Neasden House. Construction went ahead and the building was opened by Mills on Xmas day 1883, Anglican services having previously been held in rented accommodation in one of the shops.

The next step, as always, was to use the building also as a school for the children. In January 1884 Mills started a school in his house at no. 1 Kingsbury road, but was advised by a visiting schools inspector to move it across the street into the mission building, install water closets and turn it into an open elementary school with several hundred places under Government inspection and approval. The move was made and soon over half of the hundred children of school age on the estate were going to Mills's school, with a corresponding decline in numbers attending Miss Cuttrie's school in 9 Kingsbury road. Unfortunately about this time Willesden's school board got embroiled with the Whitehall education department over the larger issue of the Harlesden schools and Neasden was hit by the backwash, Whitehall insisting that schooling in Neasden must be provided by the Willesden board. Eventually after a protracted battle the Harlesden problem was resolved and in mid-1885 the Neasden school was recognised and placed under Government inspection. Of the £140 required annually for running the school £40 came from the Metropolitan and some £30 from the 'school pence' normally charged for schooling. The charges at Neasden, which were 3d a week for the eldest child in a family and 2d for each subsequent child, were lower that the Willesden average but the Metropolitan would not agree to anything higher. Unable to compete, Miss Cuttrie's school closed early in 1885; and an attempt by the Methodists to start a day school came to nothing.

The role of the churches extended beyond religious observance and education. Mills organised a library, with readingroom, and started a series of three-weekly 'entertainments' at St Saviour's which soon became a tradition. Local groups like the Neasden harmonic club and the Neasden glee class would contribute to the concerts, in which Mills was helped after his marriage in 1884 by his wife Annette, daughter of Sir William Smart KCB (inspector-general in the Navy), and by Mrs Reynolds, wife of the occupant of Fryent farm, both of whom were talented musicians. Mills and the Wesleyan leader Jonadab Finch ran separate branches of the Band of Hope and the Temperance Union, all proposals to amalgamate the rival branches being firmly resisted by the nonconformists.

Another feature of Neasden life was the double system of annual treats provided for the children of the Sunday schools. Children from the nonconformist schools of Neasden and Willesden Green were entertained each year by the Earl of Aberdeen,

ST SAVIOUR'S Quainton street: mission church and school, 1883-1945 – a sketch by the architect

who had taken the lease of Dollis hill house in 1882 in succession to his father-in-law Lord Tweedmouth, formerly Sir Dudley Marjoribanks, using it as a country retreat from his town house in Grosvenor square. Himself a nonconformist, the Earl actively supported social work in London, becoming president of the Ragged Mission in 1886 after the death of the Earl of Shaftesbury. The St Saviour's children, in contrast, had a variety of venues for their annual treat. On a July day in 1884 about a hundred of them were guests of the Rawlings family at Chalkhill house; and in the evening they marched back home in procession behind the Neasden brass band, which had been formed and equipped by Mills and was conducted on this occasion by the director of the Metropolitan railway band. In the following year they were entertained by the Goodchilds at Hillhouse farm Kingsbury.

In 1884 Mills took a momentous initiative in proposing that his territory at St Saviour's should be enlarged to take in the southern part of Kingsbury, including the ancient church of St Andrew's which had been closed for some time and which Mills now undertook to restore. The dean and chapter of St Paul's approved the idea and it went forward to the Ecclesiastical Commissioners. The result was an Order-in-Council made on 9th July 1885 which created a 'consolidated Chapelry of Neasden-cum-Kingsbury' consisting of the northern part of Willesden and the southern part of Kingsbury. It was bounded in the west by the Metropolitan railway line, in the south by the Acton branch line and in the east by the Edgware road. In the north the

Old St Andrew's Kingsbury – the parish church of Neasden-cum-Kingsbury 1885-1932; with the Finch family vault in the foreground

boundary ran from Edgware road westwards along the middle of the Brent reservoir to a point south of Wood lane, then along Wood lane to Church lane and along the footpath just north of Fryent farm to Salmon street, whence it followed the Kenton footpath north of Hillhouse farm to the Wembley parish boundary and so down to the Metropolitan railway.

It was explained in the opening sentences of the Order-in-Council that the Neasden-cum-Kingsbury parish was being created because a large population had been settled in north Willesden remote from the parish church; indeed the residents in the railway estate formed over half of the total population of the new parish, which was computed at nine hundred and thirty souls in the 1891 census. The total area of the parish was about fifteen hundred acres - the equivalent of a square with sides a little over one and a half miles long. For the remainder of Kingsbury there was a new church: Holy Innocents on high ground about a mile north of St Andrew's.

Even before the Order-in-Council was made plans were approved to erect a large new church and vicarage in Neasden on an acre of land south-east of B-street which had been acquired, with the help of the Nicols, from the Metropolitan railway. The old church of St Andrew's was very small and not used for services in the winter months but there was still the mission church of St Saviour's; so priority was given to the building of a vicarage for Mills. By July 1887 the new vicarage was ready. Built 'in an unpretentious Queen Anne style' at a cost of £1,700, it was mainly of yellow brick, with large gables breaking the roof-line. It stood well back from the road since the intention was to erect the new church in front of it.

The vicarage house-warming on 19th July 1887 was combined with the annual Sunday school treat held that year in the vicarage grounds in the afternoon. W. E. Gladstone, who had been residing at Dollis hill house for the previous five months while the Aberdeens were globe-trotting, came along to present prizes to the children and at the house-warming in the evening he gave Mills an engraving of the recent portrait of himself painted by Millais.[28] It was intended that Gladstone should plant a tree in the grounds but there was not time for this as he had to leave for his Cheshire home at Hawarden that evening by train from Willesden Junction.

On occasions such as these party politics were temporarily overlaid but they were never far below the surface and any complimentary remarks about Gladstone invariably evoked murmurs of dissent from Conservatives. A copy of a voters list for 1885 has survived in which the party loyalties professed by Willesden residents have been noted. While farmers, tradesmen and professional people naturally belonged to the Conservative camp, two out of three residents in A-street and B-street were recorded as having Liberal sympathies. The parish of Neasden, taken as a whole, could well have been split fairly equally between the two political parties. The tenant of Neasden House was exceptional in declaring, in the presence of the vicar (a Conservative), that though he was a Liberal he had voted only once in 18 years and was not likely to vote again.

Early in 1888 Mills was offered the living of St Mary's Willesden, after the resignation of the Rev.J.C.Wharton, but his heart was in his Neasden parish and he turned it down. A few months later he had a more tempting offer in the form of an exchange of livings with the incumbent of St Michael's Coventry, a large and busy parish which had been proving too much for its vicar, whose health was not robust. Again Mills at first declined but in the end he was persuaded to accept. So in the summer of 1888 James Butter arrived to take over the Neasden parish, supported by a curate (the Rev J.S.Nye) whose services Mills had obtained in the previous year with the help of the Curates Aid Society, while Mills went to one of the largest and finest parish churches in England, destined to become a cathedral in 1918 and to be destroyed in the German air raid of 14th November 1940.

Mills's work at Neasden had been outstanding. By nature energetic, genial and sympathetic, he received valuable support from the Metropolitan railway company, from the farmers of south Kingsbury, from the owners and tenant of Neasden House and from people outside his parish like the Baker family of Harlesden who helped with concerts in aid of the schools and other parish activities. In recognition of his dynamic leadership of the community during his five and a half years' incumbency Mills received a farewell gift of silverware from the parish while Neasden cricket club, of which he was founder-president, gave him a liqueur case. On the Sunday before Xmas 1888, when St Andrew's church was reopened for services after being closed for seven months for restoration, Mills came back from Coventry to preach the sermon at St Andrew's in the morning and at St Saviour's at evensong. He ran into trouble later at his new parish through trying to revive a disused church rate to supplement his stipend; in 1903 he moved to the rectory of Gedney in Lincolnshire where he died in 1909.

When Mills left Neasden in 1888 one particular problem which had arisen two years before his arrival had still not been solved. It appears that the bridge carrying the Neasden-Kingsbury road over the river Brent had not been redesigned when the Brent reservoir was constructed in the 1830s or when it was enlarged in the early 1850s. In 1881 the bridge was thirty two feet long and eleven feet wide with two brick arches each of fourteen feet resting on a central pier which formed the boundary between the parishes of Willesden and Kingsbury. Eventually the pressure of water produced at those times when the sluices were open caused the central pier to give way in April 1881.

Responsibility for repairing the bridge was said to rest equally with the lords of the manors of Kingsbury (All Souls College) and Neasden.[29] It was not obvious who the legal successor was to the lord of the manor of Neasden but it was eventually agreed that the Willesden Local Board should bear half the cost of erecting a new bridge. By a coincidence the road bridge over the Acton branch line at Dudden hill had collapsed on Boxing day 1880, requiring a temporary wooden bridge which was still in place two years later. Foreseeing an even longer delay over the rebuilding of Kingsbury bridge, the Willesden engineer Claude Robson erected in May 1881 a stout timber bridge at a cost of nearly £200, half of which was contributed by the Hendon guardians who besides administering poor-law matters also acted as the sanitary and highway authority north of the Brent.

In 1883 the Willesden board and the Hendon authorities agreed on the erection of a new girder bridge costing £969 but Hendon now jibbed at finding half of the money. The historic arrangement of equal shares still applied to the maintenance of the temporary timber bridge as late as 1891 but Hendon argued that its share of the new permanent bridge should take into account the relative wealth of the two sides. There is little doubt that the creation of the Metropolitan works and estate on the Willesden side was producing a great increase in traffic over the bridge: in the course of one week in the summer of 1887 the temporary bridge carried 2,446 pedestrians, 1,269 horses and 1,336 vehicles including 352 bicycles.

As time went by, voices were raised on all sides complaining about the hazards which the narrow temporary bridge presented. For instance the Rev. Mills was moved to write in his parish magazine:

> 'It is evident that till some member of the Hendon Highway and Sanitary Authority either breaks his own neck or has some member of his family killed at Kingsbury bridge the present disgraceful state of affairs will be allowed to continue'.

The Hendon authorities were told at one meeting in 1886 that, when a pony and chaise had fallen off the bridge a day or two earlier, the vehicle had floated downstream part of the way to Brentford. The narrow bridge was particularly dangerous because of the steep descent of the approach from the Kingsbury side. As William Memory, the former horse-bus operator at Harlesden, told his colleagues on the new Middlesex County Council in 1890, if a horse bolted down the hill it was sure to go into the river. But the county council refused even to consider the question of making a contribution towards the cost of the new bridge before it was actually built.

In the end, the Hendon authorities agreed to contribute £350 or half of the cost of a new bridge, whichever was the less, and on this basis plans were drawn up and agreed. Although the new bridge was to have the same span as the old one it was to be nearly three times as wide between the parapets, with provision for the pedestrian footways to be transferred outside the parapets on cantilever supports should an even wider carriageway become necessary later. Construction work started in August 1891 and the new girder bridge, illuminated at night by gas lamps at the four corners, was opened in January 1892, more than ten years after the collapse of its predecessor. Of the total sum of £1,400 which the bridge itself cost, exclusive of the work done on the approaches, the £350 contribution from the Kingsbury side worked out at exactly a quarter. Most of the expenditure fell in the financial year 1891–92 and the Willesden Local Board raised during that year a 'Kingsbury bridge loan' for £850 with a term of 30 years at three and a half per cent. After much delay the Middlesex authorities decided in mid-1892 to contribute £300.

As noted earlier, the Metropolitan railway estate was never in the best of physical shape, mainly because of damp. The houses had middens but all the sink and slop water flowed straight into the Brent, to the great concern of the Thames water authorities. Cesspools were created in 1886 but since 1883 there had been plans to connect the houses to a main. These plans were based on a division of Willesden into two drainage districts.

Ever since the local board came into operation in 1875 there had been arguments about whether districts should be formed within Willesden for various functions. It was argued by Jackson, an East Willesden member of the board, that it was unfair for Neasden's heavily rated farmers to have to pay for gas-lighting and water supply in which they did not share. But in reply it was pointed out that agricultural land was rated at only a quarter of the standard rate. Roads accounted for half of the local board's total expenditure and the main beneficiaries from road expenditures were the rural areas. If Neasden became a separate district it would have to find all the money for its roads from its own rate income; so it could be worse off, not better off, if separated from the rest of Willesden. After this, Jackson switched his objective to getting more work done for Neasden under the existing system and in November 1877 he presented a memorial to the board signed by Hopkinson, Prout, Burton and other Neasden notables complaining that Neasden was not getting a fair share of Willesden's expenditure. One result of this pressure was the extension of gas mains up Neasden lane as far as Burton's farm. But the most important issue was drainage.

Because of the Brondesbury ridge watershed there were naturally two separate drainage areas in Willesden. Kilburn already had its sewerage connected to the metropolitan disposal system and in 1883 the Willesden surveyor submitted a plan for draining the 'Brent' district north of the watershed. One main would follow the Brent for about two miles from near the reservoir and could be used for draining the new railway estate. Another would run from Edgware road at Cricklewood following the line of the Slade brook along Neasden valley. A third called the 'Harlesden valley' main would run in part along Dog lane. In 1884 Willesden won a legal case against the Metropolitan Board of Works (formerly called the Greek street Commissioners) who wanted to stop Kilburn draining into the metropolitan system; so the way was now clear for setting up a separate 'Brent district' system with a sewage farm on the edge of Neasden, after an earlier attempt to site it at Twyford had met with strong opposition, not least from the tenant of Twyford Abbey. In April 1886 the new works were opened on land between Dog lane and the river, extending almost to Harrow road, but it still took another two to three years and a successful prosecution of the Metropolitan railway by the Thames authorities before the railway cottages were connected to the main.

The cost of the sewage works had to be borne wholly by the Brent district in the form of an additional Brent rate. This amounted at first to 1s3d in the £, or an extra third above the level of the 'Metropolitan district' rate. The extra burden was not quite so heavy in later years but it remained substantial and was a major cause of the continued antagonism between the north and south of Willesden until it was removed in 1920.

Round Neasden green, where the big houses stood, the arrival of the Metropolitan had little immediate impact. In or just before 1880 Charles John Rotherham came to the Grange while retaining his business in South Molton street near Bond street. As a young vet he had apparently been called in to attend to the royal dogs at Windsor and when he transferred from the Grange to the Grove in or about 1885 he established a dogs home there and called it the Royal Canine Hospital, Neasden. In the late 1890s Rotherham, now 'a white-haired, florid gentleman', was still busy attending with his assistant to over a hundred dogs. The pets of the aristocracy were housed in separate 'private wards' each consisting of two small connecting rooms, while the less well-to-do patients were accommodated in 8 'public wards' containing 12 beds each; all had the benefit of a large open-air swimming bath. Curiously, Rotherham did not belong to his professional body and it is not clear what sort of reputation he had within the profession.

From 1885 the Grange was occupied by Samuel Hutchinson, MRCS, a dental surgeon with a practice in Brook street, where he probably knew Rotherham just round the corner in South Molton street, and from 1887 by W.Mattieu Williams (his mother was of Swiss extraction) who had previously lived at Stonebridge park. When he came to Neasden at the age of 67 Williams had a national reputation as a lecturer and popular writer on a wide range of scientific subjects. A fellow both of the Chemical Society and of the Royal Astronomical Society, he was science editor of the *Gentleman's Magazine* throughout the 1880s. It was while at Neasden that he wrote his intended masterpiece 'The Vindication of Phrenology' which he was revising when he died at the Grange in November 1892. His third son Alyn Williams, who achieved distinction as a painter of miniatures, exhibited a portrait of his father at the Royal Academy in 1893 and subsequently elsewhere.

But Neasden had a much more direct link with the art world during the 1880s. In 1882 the editor of the *Willesden Chronicle* tantalised his readers with the news that the new occupier of Neasden House (following the death of Prout and the departure of his sister Elizabeth to Kensington) was to be 'the gentleman who for many years has had the honour of familiarising the public with the pictures of M. Gustave Doré'. This was in fact George L. Beeforth, a Scarborough man born in 1823, who had started a bookselling business in his home town before moving to London around 1867 to go into partnership at 35 New Bond street with J. F. Fairless, son of a Scottish painter Thomas Kerr Fairless. The firm's policy was to acquire modern paintings, sometimes for large sums of money, and to publish engravings made from them.[30] Seeing one day a sketch by the French artist Gustave Doré, Beeforth commissioned him to paint pictures for the New Bond street gallery, which he modified to accommodate Doré's enormous 'Christ leaving the Praetorium'. From 1868 until his death in 1882 Doré produced a steady stream of pictures and 35 New Bond street (later Sotheby's) became known as the Doré Gallery.

In 1882 Beeforth and his wife, who had been living in Belsize park, moved into Neasden House as lessees of the Nicols. Although he had earlier served for a time on Scarborough town council and was later to be its mayor, Beeforth seems to have stood aloof both from national politics and from Willesden's local affairs, although he gave generously to Neasden school to the tune of £20 a year, subscribed liberally to the fund for the new Neasden vicarage, and provided a steady supply of flowers from his gardens for the parish church.

In 1889, when the whole stock of paintings at the Doré Gallery had been successfully engraved, Beeforth and his partner sold up and retired. Fairless died in Cairo in 1891 while Beeforth, now 66, returned to Scarborough, becoming a J.P. and in 1893–94 the town's mayor. At Scarborough he built a lot of fine property under the south cliff and, possibly encouraged by his experience at Neasden, established one of the first seaside rose-gardens. In March 1923 he received the congratulations of the monarch on becoming a centenarian and died in April 1924 as the Grand Old Man of Scarborough at the phenomenal age of 101.

In New Bond street Beeforth had as his near-neighbours two veterinary surgeons called South, father and son. Almost certainly the reason why the son William Alfred South, a horse vet, came to Neasden was that he knew either Beeforth, only five doors away, or the dog vet Rotherham round the corner in South Molton street, or both; and there was plenty of scope for a horse vet at a place like Neasden.

B: A World of Horses

In Victorian England almost all the work done later by the petrol engine was done by the horse. It pulled the plough along the furrow, the cart along the lane, the barge along the canal and the carriage, bus and dray along the street. In London there was a large and increasing demand for horse-power, for as business boomed and the middle class grew, so did the demand for horse-drawn cabs and buses. And although the new iron horse on the railway line made the long-distance stage-coach obsolete almost overnight, the railways in fact greatly increased the importance of the horse, because the more goods the trains carried into and away from the railheads, the more loads there were for horses to cope with. Every station of any size had a coal storage area where the local merchants would fill their carts for retail distribution to houses and factories; for instance the Willesden firm of E. Beckett & Co started their business in 1876 at the Duddinghill railway station, dealing in coals like 'Derby brights' brought down from the midlands on the new line to St Pancras.

A writer in 1893 estimated London's horse population at 300,000 animals.[31] Among the leading commercial users were the omnibus and tram companies and the cab-drivers. Then came the railways, especially the termini on the northern perimeter where, for example, the Midland had developed a vast trade in beer from Burton-on-Trent stored in the vaults below St Pancras station. Then there were carriers like the Post Office, Pickfords and Carter Paterson, corporation refuse-carts and an endless variety of carts and drays belonging to brewers, coal merchants and dealers in merchandise of every description. Finally there were tens of thousands of carriages, most of which were horsed by hirings from 'jobmasters'. Burton of Neasden had a jobmaster business in Marylebone high street; so, locally, did James Pearl at Neasden Cottage, while Memory and Cakebread of Harlesden, who had run the horse-buses, were in the same line of business with their 'livery stables'.

Town work was heavy and difficult for the horses. Minor earth roads were scarred with ruts and where stones and chippings were added these were often simply thrown down without being rolled in. Pulling loads over such surfaces was hard, slow work. But where flat-top cobbles produced a smoother surface horses shod with iron shoes would slip about and have almost as difficult a time. The main streets, too, were heavily congested and the constant stopping and starting, the quick acceleration and sudden braking, imposed great strain on the town horse.

Even in rural areas like Neasden life was not without hazard for horses. The lanes, always rutted, were often waterlogged; and in the early darkness of a winter afternoon the station horse-bus, guided only by the feeble light of its oil lamps (if they had not already been extinguished by the jolting of the vehicle), found it difficult to steer a middle course between the footway on one side of Church road and the ditch on the other. It is not surprising if in bad weather or during the winter the bus sometimes failed to connect with the train it was supposed to meet.

On the roads horses were easily frightened and hardly a week passed without the local newspaper reporting a scene of havoc caused by a runaway horse and the vehicle behind it. In 1888 for instance the vicar of Neasden was being driven back to his vicarage from St Andrew's when the horse took fright. The two occupants of the dogcart were thrown out and the vicar was knocked unconscious and badly bruised by the coachman falling on his chest. In Neasden lane in 1895 George W. Twyford, publican at Neasden's 'Spotted Dog', was driving an open cart with his wife when the horse bolted. George was thrown out and had to be taken to Willesden's new cottage hospital where he was detained; and only two months later his potman sustained a similar accident with the same horse. In 1891, according to the *Willesden Chronicle*, two horses going down the lane from Neasden to Church End took fright at a passing train and galloped headlong into a phaeton, smashing in the front and spilling the occupants into the roadway.[32]

Concern about the London town horse led to the first of the annual parades of cart-horses in Battersea park in 1886, the idea being that owners who wanted to take part in the parade, for which prizes were offered, would see that their animals were well looked after. In the following year Miss Anne Lindo, who lived in Maida Vale, made a lengthy appeal at the annual meeting of the RSPCA for support for a movement she had just started. She was concerned that horses belonging to small one-horse businesses were often prematurely worn out simply because they never had a short holiday from work. If for a small fee such horses could be put into a rest home for a few weeks with good pasturage and veterinary care they could be restored to full vigour, while the owner could borrow a substitute horse from the home until his own animal returned. A further idea was that aging animals for which well-to-do owners had a sentimental attachment could be allowed to live out their days in good surroundings at the home in return for a fee sufficient to produce a profit which would help to finance the main purpose of the enterprise.

At a first meeting in 1886 the name proposed was the Convalescent Home for Horses but at the next meeting this was changed to the Home of Rest for Horses. Included in the distinguished committee, as its veterinary specialist, was William Alfred South of 40 New Bond street, who had already inspected and approved a farm at Sudbury which the movement proposed to rent. South, then aged nearly forty, was admitted fellow of the Royal College of Veterinary Surgeons in the following January, doubtless on the strength of his new appointment. About the same time the Duke of Portland, Master of the Horse, became the home's president.

It was predictable that horses, like railways, would become important for Neasden. Being the first open country to the north-west of London, its high ground was as good a place for horse farms as its low ground was for railway depots; and Neasden already had a long string of names connected with the world of horses like Robert Newman, the Hall brothers, James Pearl, Burton and the Krcrouse brothers, quite apart from the up-market stud farm at Oxgate ('Willesden Paddocks') established by the famous firm of Tattersall's in 1840. There can be little doubt that it was W. A. South who, hearing about the local pastures from Beeforth or Rotherham (or both), brought the Home of Rest for Horses to Neasden.[33] According to the home's records, their first horse was put out to grass in a field at Neasden and for a time both Neasden and Sudbury were used. The income from fees was supplemented by the proceeds of special money-raising events such as the fête held at Neasden stud farm on August bank holiday 1887 and by various legacies. By this time the establishments at Neasden and Sudbury had already taken in over fifty horses and by the end of 1887 the total had risen to ninety. At Neasden, where there were about twenty loose boxes and thirty-five to forty acres of pasture, a 'fête champêtre' was held in the summer of 1888, including military sports on horseback, a cab-horse parade, a cabdriving competition and jumping events; among those present were Anne Lindo, Sir Francis Burdett (bart) of the RSPCA, several cavalry officers and of course W. A. South, who now lived at the stud farm. In this year 1888 the number of horses treated at Neasden and Sudbury rose to 156.

The following year 1889 brought changes. The home held its annual ball in May at the Hotel Metropole, the music provided as always by an army band, but two months earlier South had ceased to act as its veterinary specialist and thereafter no more horses were accommodated at Neasden. During its two years at Neasden the home had made good progress and there were plenty of cabmen who said that without it they would

William Burton's STUD FARM – earlier known as Neasdon Farm and Newman's Farm

have gone out of business. Others were grateful for advice received about the shoeing of their animals from South, an acknowledged expert on diseases of the horse's foot and well-known as the inventor of the 'Rational' horseshoe (a modification of the French 'Charlier') which won him several gold and silver medals. The home did not long remain at Sudbury, which was too far away from London, moving to Friar's-place in Acton in 1890, to Cricklewood lane in 1908, to Borehamwood in 1934 and to Speen in Buckinghamshire in 1971.

C: Neasden in the Nineties

South may have severed his connection with the horse home when he moved into Neasden House following George Beeforth's return to Scarborough in 1889. Shortly afterwards the long-standing issue of the Neasden House pew in the church was raised yet again and finally resolved. After the departure of the genial Mills in 1888 there may not have been much rapport between Neasden House and the new vicar, Butter, who was a studious man in poor health. At all events when W. E. Nicol's elder son and heir died at Kensington in April 1891 shortly before his twelfth birthday the lad was buried not locally in Kensington, nor in Scotland, nor in the new Neasden parish at St Andrew's but surprisingly at St Mary's Willesden. The brief inscription on the large

NEASDEN HOUSE - the front from the east

tombstone makes no mention of his mother and takes up only the topmost portion of the stone, as if to leave room for quite a number of future interments. In November 1891 the vicar told a committee set up to consider improvements to the church that he had been in correspondence with both Nicol the owner and South the tenant of Neasden House about removing the pew. By the middle of 1892 all had been agreed and in August the pew was finally taken away to the Nicols' house in Queen's-gate where it was adapted for domestic purposes. Notable among the non-residents who subscribed to the 1892 restoration work at St Mary's are the names of W. E. Nicol of Ballogie, the Earl of Aberdeen, G. L. Beeforth and W. E. Gladstone.

Outside his professional veterinary work South added much to the variety of life at the old centre of Neasden. He remained as Nicol's tenant when in 1893 a golf course was established on what had been Wilson's farm and Turner's farm extending up to the border with Dollis hill, with accommodation for the golf club in Neasden House. It is not clear whose idea the golf club was but it was just the sort of idea likely to occur to South himself. Another of the leaders of the enterprise was probably Stanley Clifford of St John's Wood, a good golfer who was later a frequent winner in the monthly competitions; he was secretary of the club during its first ten years and subsequently honorary secretary after a paid secretary was taken on.

In 1894 the course consisted of 18 holes, with a par of 62, and was open with caddie service seven days a week. Other attractions included tennis lawns, a large pond suitable for skating in winter and (a year later) a bowling green and croquet lawn. In the first year 200 members paid an entrance fee of ten guineas (soon reduced to five) and an annual subscription of six guineas; ladies were admitted at two guineas as associate members with restricted facilities. The hon. Alfred Lyttleton M.P. was president of the club, with Chandos Leigh (a descendant of the Brydges family) as one of the four vice-presidents, and with a committee of five including W. A. South.

The appeal of the club was not to the local inhabitants of Neasden, or even of Willesden, but to the well-to-do golfers of London's west end and north-west suburbs. A club yearbook for 1897 shows that only ten per cent of the members resided in Willesden, most of the others being from the west end of London, St John's Wood, Maida Vale and West and South Hampstead. Three of the members lived at Neasden but two of them (South and the vicar) were members on an honorary basis. The third was Samuel Lithgow, a solicitor with a business in Wimpole street in Marylebone who came to live at Neasden Cottage in the year the club was founded, succeeding James Pearl who died in December 1892.

Lithgow had almost certainly known Neasden earlier because in 1891 his mother and sister were involved in a road accident at Neasden.[32] There were others, however, who after joining the club found the neighbourhood so attractive that they came to Neasden to live. Thus the manufacturer Edwin Tubbs, who lived at West Hampstead, became tenant of the Grove in 1900 after being a club member since its foundation in 1893. And when Tubbs died in 1912 he was succeeded at the Grove by another manufacturer, George Glanfield from Canfield gardens in West Hampstead; George was almost as keen a golfer as his brother Robert who lived in Swiss Cottage and had belonged to the Neasden golf club since 1894.

By 1897 the facilities of the club had expanded. The limit on membership had been raised from two hundred and fifty to three hundred and 'country members' who resided more than ten miles from the club were admitted for four guineas a year without entrance fee. It was more than just a golf club. A card-room was available with seat fees and limits on stake money. In the billiards room games of billiards, pool and pyramids could be played at fixed rates. Board-and-residence could be had for half a guinea a day or three guineas a week and a one-night bedroom for 9s6d. Lunch was served at 2s3d and dinner at 3s6d. For those who came to the club by horse transport there was stabling for twenty horses at a charge of a shilling a horse, with 6d extra for a feed of corn.

Among those who belonged to the club not for its golf but for its social amenities was William Robertson Nicoll, founder of the *British Weekly*, who lived in Frognal in Hampstead (though a Scot from Aberdeenshire, he was no relation of W. E. Nicol or of the Nicolls of Middlesex). It was a joke among his friends that for many years after joining the club in 1894 he gave his recreation in *Who's Who* as 'member of Neasden golf club' although he was no gamesman and never played. In 1903 he transferred his allegiance to the Hampstead club, was knighted in 1909 and became a Companion of Honour in 1921.

A hobby which probably took up more of South's time and money than any other was aeronautics. Confident that a flying machine was a practical proposition, he conducted experiments in the grounds of Neasden House but the test area was so besieged with spectators eager to catch a glimpse of the contraption that he had to find another site for it. It was this interest in aerodynamics which was partly responsible for his being dubbed jocularly as 'professor' South.

There were other novelties at Neasden in the late-Victorian period than flying machines. William Morley, who laid out a huge area of playing fields near the station in the 1880s, also created a shallow open-air 'lakelet' which easily froze over in winter to provide a smooth, safe surface for skaters. Less successful was Sir Edward Watkin's plan to set up, within sight of his proposed Wembley Tower, a 1½-mile track for experiments with the French invention of the 'chemin-de-fer glissant' or gliding railway. The idea, applied with success at the Paris Exhibition of 1889, was that trains would run over a series of nozzles which, as the train passed over them, would eject spouts of water so angled as to propel the train backwards or forwards as the driver wished. The train ran in effect on skates with a thin cushion of water trapped between it and the track, rather like the air-cushion beneath a hovercraft. A contract was signed with the French company which at its own expense was to conduct the experiment but people like Sir Douglas Galton, later president of the British Association, felt that over long distances the system of propulsion would not be economic. This scepticism was shared by the Metropolitan's own engineers and in fact the experiment planned for Neasden was never carried out.

Another of South's many activities was the presidency of Neasden cricket club, following in the steps of the Rev. Mills. The club played, like so many others, on Morley's cricket ground adjacent to Dog lane which William Lansdale Morley - a local politician, representing Church End, who owned the small row of houses called Lansdale terrace in Neasden lane opposite Denzil road - had rented from the Metropolitan on a long lease in the early 1880s. The cricket club's social activities like the annual dinner and occasional smoking concerts invariably took place at Neasden's 'Spotted Dog', which was also the meetingplace for a variety of other organisations such as the Neasden musical society, the Neasden quoits club, the Finchley harriers and the Neasden cycling club.

Cycling clubs flourished in Willesden even before Dunlop's invention of the pneumatic tyre in 1888. In these pre-automobile days, before motor cars were allowed generally on the roads after 1896, the bicycle was 'king of the road'. There was no need for rear lamps and because other lights on the roads were so few a front lamp had to be lit only from an hour after sunset to an hour before sunrise. In 1885 the Willesden club, in Harlesden, had the celebrated Mattieu Williams as its president and a Neasden club, based on the 'White Hart' in Church End, had its first run of the 1887 season to Harrow. In August 1892 Neasden organised a special event in the form of a six-club 'lantern ride' round Willesden starting and finishing at the 'White Hart'. By 1895 the programme was crowded with fortnightly runs to places as far away as Windsor and Hatfield. But in 1898 the club seems to have decided to become less athletic in character, changing its name to Neasden Social Cycling Club with headquarters at the 'Spotted Dog'. With its wider appeal to both sexes the club was said to be one of the most flourishing in north-west London.

It was not only among sporting folk that the 'Spotted Dog' had a good reputation.

When members of Willesden's local board wished to celebrate privately the Queen's golden jubilee in 1887, George Twyford laid on a dinner for them, with the Willesden brass band playing festive music in the forecourt outside; and his son George William, who took over the licence from his father in about 1891, did likewise when the councillors and chief officers of the new urban district council wanted a similar private dinner to mark the twenty-first anniversary of the now defunct local board in 1896.

Meanwhile, there had been developments on the other side of Dog lane at The Model Farm. The land to the west and south of the farm buildings was sold in 1882 to Richard Richards and from 1885 began to be built on. Gradually a line of semi-detached villas appeared fronting Neasden lane and a double line of similar houses along a new road called Lansdowne grove, which completed a triangle of which Neasden lane and Dog lane were the other two sides. Later, in the diamond jubilee year 1897, a small block of dwellings called Lansdowne gardens was added fronting Dog lane but set well back from the roadway.

The Model Farm itself became exclusively a horse establishment occupied successively by the Krcrouse brothers, John Davies, Sydney Galvayne and Harold Fitzroy. Alfred and Edward Krcrouse were both born in Maidstone in mid-century to the English wife of a farmworker and horsebreaker of German origin who had become a naturalised British subject. Galvayne was a flamboyant operator and may have been Australian. When he bought the farm from James Pearl in July 1891, and when he sold it to Fitzroy five months later, he described himself as a 'professor of horsemanship'. Besides having nearly forty loose boxes for horses and a carriage repository, he ran a riding and driving school and offered services like breaking-in and pasturing. The selling-ring at the farm was sometimes used for outside sales, as when a dealer in August 1891 brought about a hundred and fifty Argentinian horses to the farm in procession along the streets from Willesden Junction.

Earlier that year the Duke of Teck paid the farm a visit accompanied by his two eldest sons, brothers of the future Queen Mary. The Duke himself had been a cavalryman and Adolphus ('Dolly') and Francis ('Frank') both had careers in the British army. Francis in particular was passionately fond of horses and it was said of him that 'no-one took as much care of his horses as he did or turned them out so well'; after his service with the dragoons he became chairman of the Middlesex Hospital's management board.

In the early 1890s, out of a desire to preserve some of the old village character of Willesden amid the rising tide of urbanisation, there was a sudden blossoming of fêtes and garden societies. In the summer of 1892 a Willesden-and-Neasden show was organised on the glebe land near the 'White Hart' to raise funds for the future Willesden cottage hospital. Twelve months later the organisation's title had expanded to 'Willesden and Neasden Flower Fruit and Vegetable Show and Sports Association', with the Duke of Teck as president and eminent patrons like the Earl of Aberdeen. In 1893 the energetic and versatile W. A. South (FRHS) became founder-president of the Neasden horticultural society, which befriended the 'Neasden' allotment association formed for Denzil-road allotment holders about the same time and supported an annual joint flower show with the Pound-lane allotment holders. The first such show was held in July 1894 at the Regency hall in Willesden a month before the main

Willesden show; South was the treasurer and the organising committee used to meet, like the horticultural society, in Neasden House.

It may seem at first sight curious that the residents and allotment holders of Denzil road identified themselves with Neasden rather than Church End. The explanation doubtless lies in the historic connexion between the old Three Corner Field, on which the houses of Denzil road, Kingsbury crescent and London terrace had been built, with Neasden House and in particular with the smaller of the Neasden House charities. This orientation of Denzil road towards Neasden was to continue well into the 20th century; and the Council's allotments, which lay on All Souls land between Denzil road and the railway, continued to be known officially as the Neasden Allotments.

PART FIVE
The Second Stage

A. 'Last Main Line'

AFTER THE FOUNDING of the golf club the most important development in Neasden in the 1890s was the arrival alongside the Metropolitan railway of the Great Central — England's last main-line railway.[34]

The idea had had a long gestation. The Manchester, Sheffield and Lincolnshire railway had been formed by amalgamation in 1847 to provide a coast-to-coast railway link across the north midlands from Merseyside to Grimsby. It also operated a Humber ferry and later steamers to the Continent. Its main traffic was in fish and coal, but a large proportion of the coal it carried was taken only to junctions with other railways which undertook the lucrative conveyance southwards to the rapidly expanding markets of the London area.

In 1872 nearly five million tons of coal came into London by rail, over three times as much as in 1862, and the MSLR wanted to get a share of the profitable London coal traffic by building a line to exploit the undeveloped resources of the south Yorkshire coalfield west of Doncaster. Acting in concert, the MSLR and the Midland railway jointly promoted a bill for building a joint line of over a hundred miles from Askern north of Doncaster to the Midland's main line at Rushton a few miles north of Kettering, with running powers for each company over stretches of the other's tracks, including the Midland's line between Rushton and St Pancras. As expected, the bill was vigorously opposed by the Great Northern, which was carrying over a million tons of coal a year into London from collieries on the eastern side of the country in Yorkshire and Durham. The bill had a torrid time in Parliament. A Commons committee in the spring of 1873 cut out the proposed new line north of Melton Mowbray and when a Lords committee shortly afterwards excised the rest of it the Midland had had enough and decided to withdraw.

Had the 1873 bill been enacted the Brent sidings of the Midland would have been used extensively by the MSLR for marshalling coal trains, some of which would have passed over the busy Acton branch line through Dudding hill. A more interesting thought is whether in this case the future Great Central would ever have come to Neasden. Probably, in the end, it would. Sir Edward Watkin, the MSLR chairman, was chairman also of the Metropolitan railway and in 1872 his heart was already set on

The Great Central railway's 'Extension to London'

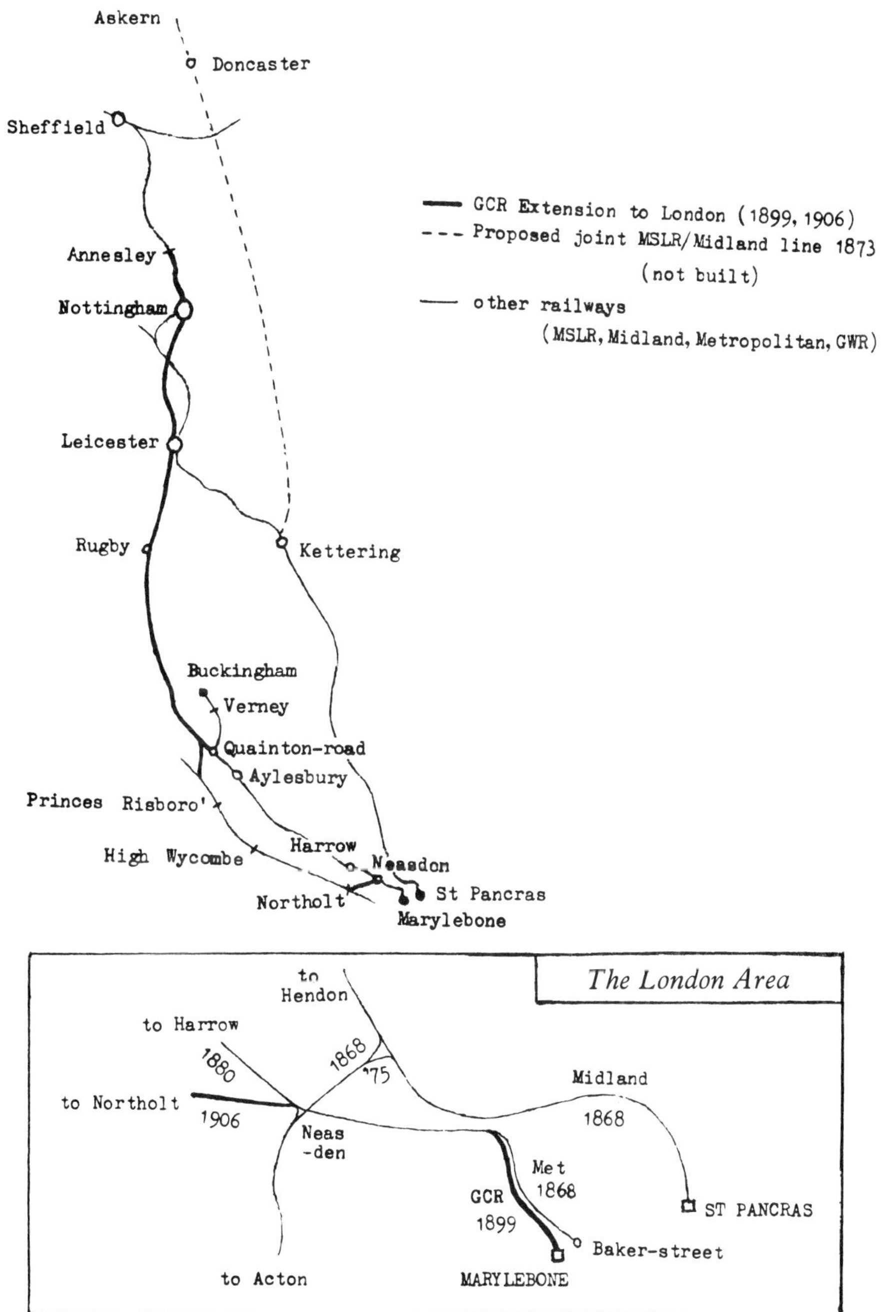

joining up his MSLR and Metropolitan systems, though this was still a long way off. The Metropolitan were to be allowed to reach a Neasden terminus in their bill of 1873 and in correspondence with the Midland's chairman in the winter of 1872–73 Watkin said quite candidly that when the time was right he would still want to join up his two railways even after the Askern-Rushton line was built.

Indeed it seems very likely that it was the failure of the 1873 Midland-MSLR joint bill which prompted Watkin to follow up his 1873 Metropolitan Railway Act so quickly with an 1874 bill to by-pass the new terminus near Kingsbury bridge and to push the Metropolitan forward to Harrow, to the great surprise of the railway world. Thereafter every mile of extension to the north-west reduced the gap between Watkin's two railway systems. By 1890 they were only a hundred miles apart and, with the Metropolitan poised to acquire the Aylesbury-Buckingham line in 1891 and to reach Aylesbury itself in 1892, Watkin now introduced a major bill for building a 93-mile MSLR 'Extension to London' from Annesley, north of Nottingham, to Quainton road station just north of Aylesbury on the line to Buckingham. The bill had a difficult passage through Parliament but was eventually enacted in 1893.* From Quainton road the MSLR would have running powers over the Metropolitan tracks as far as Canfield place (Finchley road) whence a new line would be driven through and under St John's Wood to a new terminus in Marylebone road. Using hindsight, we can say that Parliament were wrong to authorise this undertaking; but that was not the general opinion at the time.

Watkin's reasons for wanting to build this £11-million line through the centre of large towns like Nottingham and Leicester went beyond coal revenues, though these were important particularly as the midlands coalfields were the nearest, cheapest and largest suppliers of London's needs. He wanted also to get to the south coast to take advantage of the proposed Channel tunnel route to Paris and a symbol of his francophile aspirations was to be the erection on Wembley hill of a huge tower resembling the new 'Tour Eiffel' on the left bank of the Seine.

In 1895, soon after Watkin's retirement for health reasons, the MSLR started negotiating with the Metropolitan for the purchase of about a hundred and thirty acres of land at Neasden which had been bought from the Prouts in 1876. This included about sixty acres of Morley's cricket fields and another seventy acres leased to Lavender and other farmers for grazing. Agreement had seemingly been reached by correspondence in 1896 but offence seems to have been caused by the insertion of these lands in a compulsory-purchase schedule in one of the MSLR's minor bills. The correspondence became extremely acrimonious and it is not clear how the matter was finally settled. The episode is, however, typical of the frequent bickering between the two companies which occurred after Watkin had departed the scene.

In August 1897 the MSLR shed its provincial title and became the Great Central Railway. In constructing the London extension use was made of all the latest mechanical devices such as steam-powered excavators, while the locomotives and rolling stock incorporated the most advanced technology of the world's leading railway nation. Work started in earnest at Neasden in 1897 and by mid-1898 an army of navvies was reported to be working day and night to achieve the completion date with

**see Appendix VII*

the aid of huge gas flares which lit up the Neasden sky during the night shift. At almost any time during the Victorian period thousands of such navvies could find employment excavating cuttings and raising embankments. In winter they were accommodated in temporary hutments but in the summer they frequently slept in the open in the fields. At Neasden, in addition to a short row of hutments, a mission room was opened for the navvies for use as a reading-room during the week and for bible classes and services on Sundays. But there was a rowdy element given to shouting abuse at passers-by so that extra police had to be on duty in the vicinity of the new railway. Local youths imitated this rowdyism and early in 1898 there were reports of juvenile vandalism at Neasden station.

Neasden was not allowed to have a GCR station but, as the Metropolitan had found, it was a valuable site for sidings and depots. Vast quantities of spoil excavated from the new tunnels under St John's Wood were brought out by train and used to raise the level of the lowlying land south of the line, including Morley's cricket ground, some of whose turf was used to replace turf damaged at the 'nursery' end of Lord's famous cricket ground in St John's Wood. A second major railway depot now grew up at Neasden. Inside the semi-circular link with the Acton branch line, south and east of Dog lane, an engine shed was built capable of stabling thirty locomotives and Neasden became the engine depot for the London end of the GCR. To the north and west of Dog lane a large carriage repair shed was erected whose roofline could be seen from Neasden lane rising above the Dog lane bridge.[35]

The GREAT CENTRAL railway at Neasden, 1906: the lines to Harrow and Northolt, flanked by the Metropolitan-line station, showing the carriage sheds beyond the Dog-lane (North Circular road) bridge

Photograph: S.W.A. Newton

For the workshop staffs and the train crews an estate of 154 houses was built by the House & Shop Company on land leased from the GCR and the completed estate was then leased back to the railway for an annual rental of £2,100, equivalent to about five shillings a week per house. The site chosen for the estate lay south of Dog lane between the canal feeder and the newly erected fever hospital. The hospital had its first patient in 1892 in a temporary iron building but a permanent structure, purpose-built for fever cases, came into full operation in 1894. Enlarged in 1903–4 and encircled by a high brick wall in 1906, the hospital lay well outside the parish of Neasden-cum-Kingsbury and was not given the name Neasden until half a century later, though the adjoining GCR estate was described from the start as the railway's 'Neasden' estate. The pattern of hospital admissions in its first full year, when there were two hundred and fifty two cases of scarlet fever and sixty six cases of diphtheria in an overall total of about three hundred and fifty, was to prove typical for later years.

The principal road of the estate, Woodheyes road, started at the revised line of Dog lane with 4 semi-detached houses on each side, followed by another 76 terraced houses, mostly on the east side, built mainly in blocks of eight. Gresham road led off the west side of Woodheyes road immediately after the four semi-detached houses and contained 62 terraced houses, mostly on the west side, before joining up again with Woodheyes road near its southern end. The estate was completed by a row of 8 semi-detached houses called Central Villas fronting Dog lane west of Woodheyes road. Rents charged to tenants naturally included allowances for rates, maintenance and repairs, and one tenant of a terraced house remembers paying an all-in rent of 8s6d a week when he arrived in 1909. The semi-detached houses carried higher rents than the others and were initially assigned to the managerial staff, who had mostly come down from GCR headquarters in Manchester.

The name Gresham given to the shorter of the two roads was clearly derived from the Gresham family, partners in the Salford firm of Gresham & Craven which manufactured the new vacuum-brake equipment. Indeed Gresham's son had recently married the second daughter of William (later Sir William) Pollitt, the GCR manager, and some said that an equipment contract had been diverted to Gresham & Craven from another manufacturing firm because of the family alliance. But the origin of Woodheyes, which was a rare name in Lancashire and almost unknown outside the county, is not known.

The estate was no sooner completed than the GCR made the first of a long series of applications for the adoption of the roads by the Council. The Council's standard reply was that the roads must first be brought up to the standards required under the Public Health Act of 1875 and it was not until May 1915 that adoption finally took place. In the meantime this continued to be a fairly self-contained, geographically isolated community. For the children there was a corrugated-iron school in Bridge road, so called because it led under the Acton branch line to the shops beyond. In 1903 Willesden & District Co-operative Society made a bid to purchase a plot of land on the north side of Dog lane opposite Woodheyes road with a view to opening a general store for the estate. Negotiations proved difficult but in the end it was agreed that one of the semi-detached houses in Woodheyes road could be converted into a shop; so no. 7 became a shop in 1903 and remained as a shop for half a century. It seems to have been the first branch shop of the Willesden Co-op, which had been founded in 1899, and was known as the 'Cottage' branch. Postage stamps could be bought at the shop and letters posted in the pillarbox which had stood close by since 1900.

The reason why a shop was not built on the north side of Dog lane was that the GCR had plans for developing the land. The 'London extension' to Marylebone could run passenger services economically only if it could attract passengers from other lines; so fast running speeds were essential. These were ruled out, however, on the route through Harrow by the curves in the track, the gradients and incurable traffic congestion. As early as 1898 the GCR had obtained permission to build a new 6¼-mile line from Neasden to Northolt in the teeth of opposition from the Metropolitan, who foresaw a reduction in the income earned from charges levied on GCR traffic on the Harrow route.* An agreement was reached soon afterwards with the Great Western for joint running over the GWR line from Northolt through High Wycombe and Princes Risborough to Ashendon, whence a new link would run to the existing GCR main line at Grendon Underwood just north of Quainton road. Though these arrangements were finalised in the same year (1899) as the Harrow route was officially opened, the alternative route through Northolt, which was designed not only for fast expresses but also for profitable suburban traffic, with stations located at Wembley hill and beyond, did not come into full operation until 1906.

Still no GCR station was allowed at Neasden. But its freight sidings handled a vast amount of merchandise, particularly coal, and in the Edwardian period at least half a dozen coal firms had a wharf at the sidings and a coal office on the embankment in Neasden lane. At first the Northolt line diverged from the Harrow line by the side of Neasden station but later the junction was shifted to the west of the Dog lane bridge, where a large signalbox called Neasden South controlled the traffic. Neasden North was located at the far end of the sidings, near Wembley.

B: Gladstone Park and its railway

One of the environmental results of the arrival of the Great Central railway at Neasden was the loss of large areas of meadowland which had been used for cricket and football pitches including Morley's cricket ground. There was therefore very strong support at Neasden for the idea that the Council should buy from the Finch family the part of their estate which lay south of Dollis hill lane, for £50,000. The sixty seven acres lying above the Acton branch line were already laid out as parkland while the twenty nine acres below it would be eminently suitable for sports pitches. But any proposal to make a large capital outlay for the benefit primarily of the northern half of Willesden was almost bound to bring on another battle in the Thirty Years War between the north of Willesden and the south.

Some years earlier in 1894 the temperature had been lowered a little when it was decided, now that Kilburn was almost wholly built up, to extend the boundary of the North Kilburn ward to the summit of Shoot-up hill, making the ward boundary correspond with the watershed, so that the extra Brent-district drainage rate would fall

* *see Appendix VII*

only on properties actually draining towards the Brent. But the differentiated rate continued to be a burning issue and a Brent district ratepayers association was formed to press for its abolition. The question of the park gave the association as good a battleground as any for another fight with the south.

The preservation of open spaces as public parks was a question much in the air. The Queen's Park in Brondesbury had been established at the time of the golden jubilee in 1887 and was maintained by the Corporation of London. Not long afterwards in 1892 the local board had given £14,000 towards the £15,000 needed to buy the twenty six acres for Roundwood park to the north-east of Harlesden. The main opposition to the proposal to pay £50,000 for Dollis hill park was orchestrated by the editor of the *Willesden Chronicle* from his office in south Kilburn. It was, he declared, a 'wanton wicked waste'. Not only was it too far from the centre of Willesden's population (though in fact its southern edge was little more than half a mile from the parish church); it was far too big an area anyway. An odd feature of the controversy was that the strongest opposition was drummed up among Harlesden folk, who seem to have quite forgotten the boon recently conferred on themselves by the acquisition of the park at Roundwood.

At the inquiry held by the inspector from the Local Government Board the supporters of acquisition pointed in particular to the rapid growth of the 'Brent' part of Willesden, where the population had doubled in seven years, compared with an increase of just over forty per cent in the 'Metropolitan' part. The park would also be well served by railways, particularly from the busy stations of Willesden Green and Neasden; and no less a figure than Sir Henry Campbell-Bannerman, Liberal leader in the Commons, had recently expressed support for the scheme in his speech at the re-opening of Willesden cottage hospital.

The inquiry inspector recommended, as expected, in favour of acquisition. Middlesex County Council agreed to put up £12,500 towards the cost, London C.C. £3,000, Hampstead £1,000 and Hendon £500, while the Ecclesiastical Commissioners made a £5,000 loan available on easy terms. But staunch Conservatives found extremely distasteful the Council's decision to call the park after W.E. Gladstone. In May 1901, four months after the death of Queen Victoria, the park was formally opened but there was nearly a last-minute hitch. The Earl of Rosebery, recently twice prime minister, who had promised to perform the opening ceremony, was prevented from attending by the death of his mother, the Duchess of Cleveland, and the park was declared open by the Earl of Aberdeen, accompanied by Campbell-Bannerman (a future prime minister) and representatives of Willesden and other councils.

People at the time might reasonably have supposed that the new park would ensure the future of the railway which ran through it and whose station was sited within a stone's throw of its southern corner. On the opening day Harlesden folk were reported to have come to the park by rail 'crowded into the guard's and luggage vans of the tiny train to Dudden hill'. But the key word in the newspaper report was 'tiny'.

From the outset the true purpose of this stretch of railway was the conveyance of goods. But since Parliament might well reject a railway bill if the local inhabitants, while having to endure the noise, dirt and smell of the trains, were to be given no compensating benefit in the form of a station with passenger trains, it was usual for the promoters of a railway bill to provide, however reluctantly, for the running of a passenger service. Such a service was indeed envisaged in the 1864 Act for the Hendon-Acton line but when it was opened in 1868 it was for goods only and it was not until the 'Cricklewood south curve' was added under later legislation that a passenger service was introduced in 1875. Thereafter there was endless argument between the company, who complained that the passenger service did not pay, and the public who argued that it could only be made to pay if it were first improved. One serious disadvantage was that the Dudding hill station was in quite the wrong place. For the next thirty years this station remained 'in the middle of nowhere', its complete failure to attract housing to its vicinity being in sharp contrast to the numerous houses which sprang up around the Harrow-road station a mile away at Stonebridge park. Local Board figures of people living near the Stonebridge park station show how the population grew there over a period of twenty seven years:-

	Within ¼ mile	*Within ½ mile*
1865	27	114
1875	513	1,241
1892	3,672	10,874

In mid-1888 the Midland withdrew the passenger service and immediately Harlesden commuters started a campaign for its restoration. Recent cases heard before the Railway (later Railway and Canal) Commissioners had resulted in companies being ordered to reinstate passenger services which had been unilaterally withdrawn, pleas of uneconomic operation being countered with arguments that people had built houses near the stations relying on the continued availability of rail transport; that the passenger service was an integral part of the package approved by Parliament; that the uneconomic passenger trains should be cross-subsidised out of the handsome profits made from freight; and finally that the branch services brought in more passengers for the main-line trains. After a year or two the Willesden local board became interested and brought in the Hendon local board representing Cricklewood travellers.

The two boards presented their case to the commissioners late in 1892 and the main hearing was held on two days in mid-1893. The principal witness who was to have rebutted the case advanced by the railway was prevented by illness from attending and the hearing was adjourned 'sine die'. The presiding judge, however, made it clear that the court expected the two parties to reach a compromise settlement by themselves. Indeed the Midland, seeing how the wind was blowing, anticipated the outcome of the case by restoring a passenger service in May 1893, though there were still disagreements to be resolved about whether the trains should run further east than Child's hill or further south than Stonebridge park. For nine more years a skeletal service was kept alive, but only just. One railwayman later recalled that in 1902 it consisted of only one train shuttling back and forth to Gunnersbury known as the 'Crab and Winkle'.[36] Even that stopped on 1st October 1902 and this time the decision was not seriously contested.

Rather ironically the passenger service was abolished just when the volume of traffic was at last beginning to improve. In 1875 passenger traffic from Dudding hill station was meagre because there were few houses near it and access to the station was not exactly convenient. Nevertheless passenger traffic had more than doubled between 1876 and 1879 when the Metropolitan all but destroyed it in August 1880 by opening the Kingsbury-and-Neasden station, taking away all the demand from residents in Church End. Even the Stonebridge park station felt the draught, as the following figures show:[37]

	Numbers of passengers booked at:-	
	Dudding hill	*Harrow road (later Stonebridge park)*
1876	6,145	7,879
1879	13,771	20,991
1880	5,448	13,173
1881	1,247	6,116

Thereafter passengers booking at Stonebridge park were always about five times as numerous as those booking at Dudding hill but traffic increased strongly at both stations after 1900, boosted in the case of Dudding hill by the opening of Gladstone park in May 1901:

	Numbers of passengers booked at:-	
	Dudding hill	*Stonebridge park*
1900	3,583	24,790
1901	5,301	27,744
1902 (9 months):		
actual	5,150	23,134
annual rate	6,867	30,845

But the Midland company's mind was already made up. After September 1902, apart from a few through passenger trains including excursion and other specials, the line was used solely for goods traffic. The final irony was that about six years later Dudding hill station was surrounded by the Dudden hill housing estate and 'Dollis hill' station was opened on the Metropolitan line.

C: Neasden Power Station

In the same year 1902 the Metropolitan took an important step forward by getting permission to build a large generating station on the edge of its Neasden depot which would allow the whole of its rail system to run on electric power. In the bill presented to Parliament there was evidently a section which would have allowed the Metropolitan to draw water for cooling purposes from the Brent. But one of the chronic problems besetting the Brent, as everybody knew, was the irregularity of its water-flow. Less than a year previously, Willesden's medical officer had told a lecture audience that 'in the summer months the main stream of the Brent below the Welsh Harp ceases to exist', whereas in winter, with the reservoir sluices open, the torrent of water would submerge the road bridges and cause damage along the river-banks. Willesden Council promptly took steps to petition against the bill and only desisted after the Metropolitan had undertaken to remove the offending clause.

It is not clear why the clause was included in the bill in the first place because the engineers knew perfectly well that the power station would need an assured supply of water either from a water supply company or from specially sunk wells of their own. The decision went in favour of wells and two were sunk in the second half of 1902 with satisfactory results. The used water from the cooling towers was to be stored in a lake or pond between the river and the canal feeder, with a facility for releasing surplus water into the river. A proposal by the Metropolitan to have the feeder running through the storage lake, simultaneously cooling the stored water in the lake and warming up the feeder water downstream, came to nothing as the canal company proposed to levy charges which were much too high for the Metropolitan's liking. It turned out that each of the two artesian wells singly could meet the total water demands of the power station and a third was not needed until 1922.

During 1903 there were fears in the railway workers estate that the smaller maintenance needs of the new electric trains would cause unemployment. However, the manpower needs of the power station itself were clearly going to be substantial and the company now decided to build a third street of houses in the estate. A-street and B-street had been adopted by the Council in 1901–2 and were now given the names of

Metropolitan Railway workers houses in Aylesbury street and Kingsbury road (Neasden Lane North), with Gravel Pit Farm (right), c.1910

Quainton street (after the Quainton road station north of Aylesbury) and Verney street (after Verney junction on the Aylesbury-Buckingham line, named after the local landowner).

In 1904 the Metropolitan decided that the third street should consist of forty identical houses in four blocks and be called Aylesbury street. The new houses would carry rents about half as high again as the standard terraced houses in the other streets because they would have more rooms at the back, though the back gardens would be rather shorter. By March 1905 the vicar's wife could write to her cousin that the new street was already filling up fast.

Other steps taken by the Metropolitan at the same time to expand its housing stock included a decision to convert two or more of the Kingbury-road shops into wholly residential houses — a decision presumably encouraged by the fact that neither no. 1 nor no. 3 seems ever to have been used as a shop. By 1906 the first three in the row had apparently been converted, while nos. 4 to 10 were occupied respectively by a confectioner, a café proprietor, a greengrocer, a draper (with post office), a butcher, a grocer and a beer retailer. The Methodists had to give up no. 6, which had been their mission room, but they were offered instead a piece of ground on a temporary basis at the corner of Verney street and an increase in financial support from £10 a year to £25. An iron building erected on the new site continued in use until 1928 for chapel services and as a Sunday school for the children. Higher up the road, past Aylesbury street, two pairs of semi-detached houses were put up for the managerial staff at the power station, bearing the numbers 21–24; the ten numbers 11–20 Kingsbury road were left unused, presumably in case houses were later put up between Verney street and Aylesbury street. The rents for these semi-detached houses were 11s6d a week (£30 a year) including rates, compared with 8s6d a week for the new terraced cottages in Aylesbury street.

The new power station allowed the first public electric train to run on New Year's Day 1905, making travel on the railway much cleaner than in the days of steam, particularly in the tunnels. But the environmental price which Neasden residents had to pay was high. As early as March 1903 the vicar's wife foresaw in a letter that the 200-foot chimney would not prevent the pollution of people's houses and gardens; and her forecast was right. No sooner had the power station come into operation than complaints arose on all sides about the smoke nuisance. Part of the difficulty was that the sort of coal which was best for the furnaces also created a particularly dense black smoke, laden with grit. In mid-1905 the magistrates made an order requiring the Metropolitan to abate the nuisance within a period of two months and this period of grace had already expired when a strong letter appeared in the *Times* newspaper written by the eminent architect W.D. Caröe from the Athenaeum club:

> 'This power station has been erected close to Neasden station and has, of course, its large smoke stack. Day in, day out and I suppose night in, night out, this belches forth a vast volume of the blackest smoke, casting its cloud even in the clear summer air for miles around. The amount of unconsumed carbon released into the air must be prodigious and the pleasant countryside upon which the powerhouse abuts is becoming blackened and ruined. Travelling yesterday on the Great Western railway

I could see the cloud of smoke from Acton. I have seen it extending over Harrow-hill when the wind was favourable.'

In the next issue a Harlesden man commented:

> 'I had occasion to pass close to the stack when it was emitting inky smoke and as the wind was blowing from it to me I had the misfortune to experience the full benefit of the sooty grit and poisonous vapours which it was then discharging.'

A Met-line passenger with experience of industrial chimneys elsewhere wrote to say

> 'The smoke is of the blackest and thickest and continuous. The smoke issues from the top of the chimney in an almost solid condition looking as if it could be cut with a knife and, carried by the wind, it extends like a dense black cloud for at least a mile and the once pleasant rural prospect is utterly destroyed . . . I have been accustomed to the chimneys of south Staffordshire but I never saw anything there worse than the Neasden smoke stack.'

At the same time the Willesden authorities were being bombarded with letters of complaint from local residents including the occupant of the Grove who said that considerable damage was being done to his house and garden, while Neasden golf club was suffering severely. Hendon council, too, chimed in, since the smoke normally drifted towards Hendon in the prevailing wind. Proceedings were taken against the railway company early in October 1905 and the magistrates imposed the maximum penalty for non-compliance with the earlier order. As technology improved the smoke nuisance diminished, but it remained a source of local complaint until conversion to oil-firing soon after the 1939–45 war.

D: Around Neasden Green

Round Neasden green there were quite a few changes around the turn of the century. After about twenty years' residence in Neasden Charles John Rotherham left the Grove to live in St John's Wood; his business in South Molton street continued up to his death in 1922 and beyond. His successor at the Grove was Edwin Tubbs, a partner in the firm of Tubbs & Farey who were brass-founders, ironmongers and makers of upholstery springs, with one factory in Birmingham and another close to Tottenham court road. A man with a warm heart and kindly manner, Tubbs belonged to the ratepayers' association for his local ward Church End and was for two or three years its president. In March 1912 he was recovering by the sea at Brighton from severe influenza when he died unexpectedly. At his funeral at St Andrew's Kingsbury the golf club, where he had been a member since 1893, was represented by the secretary and the captain.

In 1902 Samuel Lithgow left Neasden Cottage to live at Harrow and after a few years was succeeded at the Cottage by Alex Baird-Carter, a fine-art dealer with a

NEASDEN GREEN, with the Stud Farm (right), the Grange (left) and the Spotted Dog in the distance

business in Jermyn street. Lithgow was later living near Hyde park when he represented St Pancras West on the LCC from 1910 to 1913; he was awarded a CBE in 1928 for his work on the post-war unemployment problem in Marylebone and died in 1937.

More important were the events which followed W.A. South's departure from Neasden House in 1897. South himself continued in business as a vet both in New Bond street and in his branches in Berkeley square and Paddington. In 1899 he had the distinction of being elected fellow of the Aeronautical Society but in 1907 he died at his house in Clarges street at the early age of 58 and was buried in the family grave in Paddington cemetery. Among the reasons given for his death was exhaustion, brought about no doubt by his over-enthusiastic pursuit of many diverse interests. The reasons for his leaving Neasden in 1897 are obscure but may have been connected with his health.

When South left Neasden House the tenancy was taken over by Henry Jeremiah Roberts who had been the proprietor of the St James's restaurants in two locations in the West End. Roberts allowed the horticultural society to use Neasden House for its annual soirée early in 1898 but from this time the monthly meetings were held in the vestry hall in Church End. In November 1897 the joint winner of the golf club's monthly bogey competition was a recent recruit H.H. Tankard, who lived at Watford. About a year later Tankard bought the proprietorship of the golf club from Roberts along with the goodwill, fixtures, fittings and leases of the house and grounds. But for some years he had been living beyond his means, spending large sums of money on card games, speculative investments and a mistress he maintained in Curzon street; and within three months of becoming proprietor of the golf club he was in the bankruptcy court.

The bankruptcy case marked the end of the first period of the golf club's existence. Up to then the club had been proprietary, the members having no liabilities beyond their subscriptions. Now the club was reconstituted with the name of 'New Neasden Golf Club' and financial responsibility lay with the membership. Stanley Clifford, one of the original founders in 1893, remained as honorary secretary and was probably the guiding hand in the creation of the new régime. One sign of a new policy and a new vigour at the club was the appearance of the results of the monthly and other competitions in the column of golf-club news every Monday in the *Times* newspaper; another was the warning 'club full' in the description of the club in the golfing yearbooks.

Although Clifford was to continue as honorary secretary of the club even after he left St John's Wood to live in Laleham-on-Thames in 1908, the routine secretarial work was done from 1903 by a succession of salaried secretaries. The first of these was one of the leading figures in contemporary English sport, second only to W.G. Grace as a batsman on the cricket field. Andrew Ernest Stoddart, born in South Shields in 1863 and known to his friends as 'Stod', came to London with his father and went to school in St John's Wood.[38] He made a great reputation as an attacking batsman, playing club cricket for Hampstead, and was soon in the Middlesex side. He won international caps for England at both rugby and cricket and led England to a 3–2 'Ashes' victory in Australia in 1894–95, during which tour the term 'test matches' was first applied to these contests. However, his next tour ended in a 4–1 defeat and he played little county cricket after 1900.

Stoddart was not unknown in Willesden, whose bowlers he had hammered to achieve a century in 1882 and a double century of 238 in 1887. Getting the Neasden golf club job in 1903 gave him the opportunity to develop his aptitude and liking for golf, so effectively that he quickly established a new amateur record for the course. When in 1906 the 18-hole course, which had had a relatively low par of 62, was lengthened by over a thousand yards Stoddart immediately set an amateur record for it of 75 strokes, though this was beaten by one stroke in the following year. He was also in considerable demand as a coach. Indeed so keen did he become on the game that on the day of his marriage in October 1906 in a St John's Wood church he played golf at Neasden in the morning with the vicar and the organist; and although he resided in St John's Wood the register records his profession as 'secretary' and his address as 'Neasden golf club'.

Stoddart's name must have been one of the great attractions at the Neasden club; equally he must have made an impression as a secretary because in 1907 he left Neasden to become secretary of the prestigious Queen's club in Baron's court, home of the University rugby match and numerous tennis tournaments. But he had to give up games because of 'tennis elbow' and in 1914 had to retire altogether because of ill health. Depressed by inactivity and in financial difficulties because of the war, he shot himself in his St John's Wood home in 1915. It may not be entirely a coincidence that Stoddart's death occurred less than a year after his famous old colleague Albert Trott, formerly of Middlesex and England and latterly afflicted by dropsy, committed suicide at his lodgings in Denbigh road, Willesden.

E: The London End

In considering how things developed in Neasden parish during the Edwardian period it helps to ask why its population doubled from 1,040 in 1901 to 2,074 in 1911, while there was virtually no increase in the neighbouring parish of Kingsbury (Holy Innocents). Substantially the answer is to be found in the number of new houses built. If we take the 44 houses added to the Metropolitan workers' estate, 32 built in Prout grove, 20 in Gladstone park gardens (near where the Acton branch railway line goes under Edgware road), 3 at the western end of Dollis hill lane on the south side and 119 in the Dudden hill estate just north of the railway, we already have well over 200 houses and these alone could account for almost all the population increase of 1,034.

Much the largest of the new developments was at the southern extremity of the parish where the tide of population expansion from London finally swept over the top of Dudden hill and across the railway into the Sherrick-green valley. The history of the Dudden hill estate is curious. As early as 1899 plans were drawn up for a grid of fourteen roads on the north face of the hill with names starting with the letters A to O excluding J (i.e. Aberdeen, Burnley, Cullingworth, Dewsbury, Ellesmere, Fleetwood, Geary, Hamilton, Ilkley, Kendal, Lancaster, Mulgrave, Normanby, Oakworth) but there were two related difficulties affecting the project. One was the level crossing which carried the footpath from Cricklewood over the railway towards Dudden hill lane by the side of the Slade brook. This had always been dangerous and if a public park were established adjacent to the crossing and if a housing estate were built overlapping it it would have to be replaced either by a subway or by a bridge. Discussions in 1899 between the railway and the Council were at first in terms of subways giving access to the new park but no firm conclusion was reached. The other difficulty was the brook itself which would need to be culverted.

Eventually the estate was built without Ilkley and Oakworth roads and the period 1907–10 saw the completion of Normanby road, Mulgrave road and the seventeen houses called Dollis Villas lining Dudden hill lane between Mulgrave road and the railway bridge. By 1911 a Dudding Hill Estate Association had been formed with about 200 members, a committee consisting of one member from each road and an annual budget of about £20; and the parish curate the Rev E. Crellin, residing at first at no. 17 Dollis Villas at the corner of Mulgrave road, was on the spot to provide spiritual support for an estate which sheltered about a quarter of Neasden's parishioners. Meanwhile, correspondence still flowed between the Council and the railway about replacing the level crossing. In May 1910 the Council suggested 'a subway or other such means' but by July they were proposing a 'stairway'. In 1913 an ugly iron stairway was erected slightly to the east of the former level crossing at a cost of £1,180, towards which the Midland railway made a capital contribution of £180 besides undertaking to see to its maintenance.

Housing development at Dudden hill, Prout grove and elsewhere in the south of the parish meant that over half of Neasden's parishioners now lived more than a mile away from the old parish church of St Andrew beyond the Brent. Fortunately Neasden's third vicar was well able to cope with the problem. Born in India in 1863, George Haughton Ayerst graduated at Cambridge before becoming a curate in Islington in 1890. When he came to Neasden at Easter 1898 he brought to the leadership of the parish a dynamism which had not been evident during the ten-year incumbency of his predecessor apart from the founding of an infants school in 1893. There was immediately a shake-up at the schools while W.E. Nicol renewed his interest in the parish, making frequent visits on special occasions such as the concert held in aid of the organ fund in March 1900 when Samuel Lithgow of Neasden Cottage, one of the vicar's most active supporters, described Nicol as 'practically lord of the manor'. Not long afterwards Lithgow led a deputation, including Nicol and the vicar, to the Metropolitan railway manager with a proposal to build a new school and to convert the existing one into a workmen's institute: if the Metropolitan would give an acre of land, Nicol would give £500 for a house for the headmaster. But they were not successful.

As soon as the plans for a Dudden hill estate became known it was clear how wise the church had been not to hurry to build the new parish church for Neasden next to the vicarage. It would clearly now have to be sited further south-east, preferably at the old centre of Neasden where the roads converged. In order to make temporary provision for the London end of the parish an iron church dedicated to St Catherine was put up in the angle of Prout grove (north side) and Neasden lane as a chapel-of-ease to St Andrew's, the necessary funds being supplied by Catherine Nicol and her husband. Soon after the consecration by the bishop of Islington, the very popular men's service held on Sunday afternoons was transferred to it from St Andrew's. This service, with its large orchestra, was very much the creation of Ayerst's curate and brother-in-law, the Rev E.S.B. Whitfield, a man of decidedly radical and anti-feminist views who lived at Sussex lodge in Prout grove. So popular was the service in the new location that the church had to be enlarged, by subscription, in 1903.

St Catherine's may have benefited from the proximity, just across the road, of the 'Spotted Dog' which continued to be a great centre for meetings of all kinds. For almost all of the Victorian period the Twyfords had held the licence. Joseph Twyford (1776–1860) was licensee at the Willesden Green 'Spotted Dog' for some thirty years before taking on the Neasden 'Dog', from which he retired in the latter part of the 1840s, being then about 70 years of age. By 1860 the Neasden licence was in the hands of George Twyford who retired in 1891 in favour of his son George William, destined to be the last of the Twyford publicans. When he died at the early age of 42 the first part of the funeral ceremony was held in St Catherine's iron church opposite and the interment at St Andrew's. Most of the local clubs were represented at the church or at the graveside and, as the hearse passed by, houses had their blinds down and all the shops were closed in Kingsbury road. This was probably the most notable funeral in Neasden since that of Joseph Nicoll half a century earlier. Old George Twyford died at Ramsgate in 1906, aged 78.

THE SPOTTED DOG, Neasden

So ended the Twyford tradition at the 'Spotted Dog', where the licence was subsequently held in fairly quick succession by A. Tappenden, A.W. Ferris and C.A. Hiscox until Christopher Percy began his long reign shortly before the 1914 war. Another old Neasden tradition, that of the Jackmans at the forge, survived the death of Henry at the age of 64 in 1906 and was to last as long as the forge itself. When the smithing business started to decline the Jackmans became the local newsagents.

Medical men of various kinds crop up frequently in Neasden's history. After the surgeons Pott and Holt, the vets Rotherham and South and the doctor-dentist Hutchinson, there arrived at the Grange in 1904 Edward S. Langworthy, a surgeon and physician who had previously been connected with Hutchinson's old professional address in Brook street, W.1. Langworthy's name was henceforth frequently in the news as a result of attention he gave to cyclists injured in road accidents at Neasden. He was connected with the armed forces at Hendon as a civilian consultant but he fades into oblivion after 1912. Another notable doctor was Henry C. Procter, a surgeon-doctor who had practised for many years in South Africa before returning to England to live first at Bexhill and later in Prout grove, Neasden, where he died in 1910. He was buried locally at St Andrew's and when St Catherine's brick church was built a few years later his family gave a pulpit in his memory.

The development of the London end of the parish meant that action had to be taken about this new permanent church for Neasden. In 1907, a year after the Rev. Whitfield left Neasden to become vicar of Deptford, a church hall was opened in Neasden lane

The FORGE, Neasden; the Jackman family outside their smithy and cottage

just below the forge. This made things easier for people at the London end who belonged to the many flourishing societies the parish now had, including branches of the Mothers' Union and the Girls' Friendly Society and a company of the church lads brigade. These current activities and future needs were described in a short history of the parish written by Ayerst for the bishop of London in 1907 and revised later after plans for the new church started to be discussed in earnest in 1910.

Beyond the south-western boundary of the parish the Great Central railway colony, while roughly of the same size as the Metropolitan estate, was a different sort of community. It was not in itself the nucleus of a parochial population, being within the parish of St Mary's Willesden, and did not receive the same sort of attention as the Metropolitan estate either from the church or from the parent railway company which from its remote headquarters in Manchester used to leave its estates, once set up, to their own devices.

Efforts to start a mission church for the colony made slow progress and in January 1900 the vicar of St Mary's in a printed report publicly expressed his disappointment at the poor response made to the appeal fund by the company's shareholders. The 'Dog lane mission' was at first accommodated in a hut in the field next to the engine sheds which had previously been used as a messroom and toolshed for the navvies building the railway. The room was lit with oil lamps, heated by a smelly oil stove and furnished with a wheezy harmonium and with wood forms for seating. The services were poorly attended, less because of the physical drawbacks than because of inadequate pastoral effort.

It was not until the Rev. E.B. Digby came to live close by near the end of the Edwardian decade that things changed. Under his genial leadership the mission room was frequently full for the Sunday services, the Sunday school flourished and social clubs, work groups and a strong troop of Boy Scouts were formed. It was now possible to revive an earlier plan for a new corrugated iron and matchboard building at the junction of Woodheyes and Gresham roads near the pillarbox. In the spring of 1910 the princess Marie-Louise of Schleswig-Holstein cut the first sod on the site and two months later the new church was consecrated in the name of St Raphael. This particular dedication was chosen because the saint had accompanied Tobias on his journey and this service was thought to resemble that performed by the train crews in safely conveying their passengers.

Naturally there was plenty of rivalry between the two railway estates at Neasden, especially at football and cricket. For instance a 'needle' football match used to take place every Good Friday between the GCR and the Met on a field beside Dog lane, at which music was provided by the joint GCR-Met band. The Met had had a brass band during the 1880s; if this still existed in 1900 it was then absorbed into the new joint band which at first held practices under the sonorous arches of the Dog lane bridge over the railway.

One of the milestones in the band's history was playing in Gladstone park on Edward VII's coronation day in July 1902, when the Willesden Junction band performed similarly in Roundwood park. A difficulty arose, however, when it was proposed to pay the band to give regular Sunday performances in the park in summertime, because the Council was not permitted to use the rates for this purpose. A way was found round the difficulty by allowing the band to charge the public for chairs and programmes but eventually the Local Government Board in Whitehall softened its view and allowed the rates to be used for the band, which now got a seasonal fee of £35 for the Sunday recitals, increased to £50 when Thursday (early closing day) performances were added later. The band entered many competitions, notably the annual Crystal Palace contests from 1904 onwards, and was soon able to add the word 'silver' to its title. In 1911 the band gave another special recital in Gladstone park to honour the coronation of George V and in 1923 achieved its highest distinction by winning second prize at Crystal Palace.

The band was not the only extra amenity added to the park over the years. In the summer of 1903 the Earl of Aberdeen opened a concrete-lined open-air swimming pool, holding nearly half a million gallons of water, close to the Neasden entrance. There was of course no mixed bathing in those days. Saturdays, Sundays and Mondays were free but on other days there was a 3d. charge, except on Wednesdays — a day reserved for females — when the 3d. charge applied only in the forenoon. By the end of the Edwardian period 10,000 bathers a year were using the pool.

Other sports flourished in the park. Over 3,000 people a year paid 2d. an hour to use the bowling greens and over 5,000 played tennis at 4d. an hour, while a dozen football clubs and two dozen cricket clubs paid two guineas a season for pitches below the railway. At one period the Council tried to augment its income by using part of the park to graze sheep but fencing was a problem and the practice was soon abandoned.

A bigger source of income which the Council managed to retain for over five years was the continued letting of Dollis hill house to the newspaper owner Sir Hugh Gilzean-Reid. But the Middlesex county council understandably objected that they had not provided a quarter of the purchase price of the park to watch the Willesden council let off part of the asset and pocket the rent. So the lease was not extended after the end of 1906 and the Gilzean-Reids moved to Tenterden in Hendon, bringing to an end forty years of Scots-Liberal occupation at Dollis hill.

At the other end of Neasden, beyond the fever hospital, the future of the sewage farm was becoming increasingly doubtful. When created in 1887 it had occupied twelve acres but such was the growth of population in the 'Brent' district of Willesden that ten years later it covered ninety acres. Unemployment was a serious problem in Edwardian times and in 1907 Willesden's 'Distress Committee' took advantage of grants offered under the Unemployed Workmen Act of 1905 to do £2,500 of work on the sewage farm filters. But by 1908 it was generally accepted that the sewage farm had been a shortsighted idea and that quite a different system was now needed. In 1911 the farm stopped treating sewage, which was henceforth pumped into the LCC system. However, the LCC sewers could not cope with the Brent district's surface waters; so the old sewage farm remained in existence but with the limited function of channelling surplus surface water into the river.

PART SIX
The Final Surge

A. The First World War

ALTHOUGH the outbreak of the 1914 war caused much disruption and change at Neasden, as it did everywhere, two major building projects went ahead in the early months. One was a large new school in Bridge road for the children of the GCR estate and the surrounding area, which was completed and opened in 1915. The other was the new permanent St Catherine's church.

The effort to raise funds for the new church began in 1910. Mr and Mrs Nicol gave up half an acre of land from the grounds of Neasden House at the corner of Dollis hill and Dudden hill lanes (part of the land illicitly enclosed by Sir William Roberts in the 1650s) and the exact position of the building was marked out on the ground, but construction had not begun when within the space of four months both of the Nicols died. W.E. Nicol died suddenly at Ballogie two weeks after the outbreak of war and was cremated at Kincardine O'Neil on Deeside. Catherine made her will a month later at Ballogie before returning to Kensington where she died on 18th December 1914, aged 66. Within three days her body was interred in the parish churchyard of St Andrew's at Kingsbury, the Rev Ayerst officiating.

Obscurity surrounds the relationship of Catherine Nicol with Neasden after the death of her father in 1881. She liberally supported the new Neasden parish formed in 1885 but although her husband and her daughter Dorothy frequently visited Neasden during Ayerst's incumbency in support of parish events there is nothing to suggest that Catherine herself ever came to Neasden after 1881. She must have been pained by the reckless assertion made in public at the Willesden Vestry in 1888 (later published in the local newspaper) that she was failing to distribute annually the Neasden House charities founded in the 17th century, when in fact she was doing this in a most exemplary manner in liaison with the Charity Commissioners.* Lawyers exchanged letters and the affair blew over; but it doubtless left its mark.

For no apparent reason Catherine, though she was never a parishioner of the new Neasden parish and had been married at St Mary's in 1873, was not buried in the same grave as her eldest son Malcolm at St Mary's but in a new grave at St Andrew's, presumably on the strength of an understanding with the vicar and members of her family in London, there being no burial instructions in the will. But even more curious

* *see Appendix III, c*

is the fact that, while Catherine's death was noted in the London *Times* and the Aberdeen papers, not a word about her death or her funeral appeared in the local newspapers, though plans for the new brick church to be built in her memory had been well publicised for the past four years and the site was already staked out. The local press had been similarly silent when Malcolm died. Catherine died of heart failure. But she had also had bulbar paralysis for a year and could have suffered from some sort of incapacity for longer. More than this we are never now likely to know.

In February 1915 Dorothy Nicol turned the first sod on the site of the altar for the new church and three months later the foundation stone was laid. As Prince Arthur of Connaught, president of the Neasden golf club, was prevented by war duties from performing the ceremony, the stone was laid by Captain Randall James Nicol, Malcolm's younger brother, who was convalescing after being wounded in France. On Saturday, 4th March 1916 — the 68th anniversary of Catherine's birth — when all but the western section had been completed, the church was consecrated by the bishop of the diocese. Among those present were the architect of the building J.S. Alder, the creator of many Middlesex churches including St Michael's Cricklewood, and the commandant of the newly opened military hospital at Dollis hill house, with many of her staff and some of her patients. At a reception held afterwards at the church hall in Neasden lane the veteran Samuel Lithgow, always an ardent worker for the parish in the ten years he lived at Neasden Cottage, proposed the vote of thanks to the visitors.

At the time of the 1916 consecration the seating capacity of the church was 520, about two-thirds of the planned total of 760 seats, with ninety feet of the overall length of a hundred and thirty feet completed. The pews in the nave and side-aisles were donated by Elizabeth Prout, Catherine's aunt, who lived on at Paddington to the age of ninety two and was buried by Catherine's side at Kingsbury in 1918. The pulpit was given by Mrs Procter in memory of her husband and of her son, formerly captain of Neasden church lads brigade, who fell in Flanders in 1915. The communion rails were the gift of the congregation of St Andrew's in memory of Edith Cavell and within the sanctuary twin sedilia were given by Randall Nicol. An outdoor pulpit in the churchyard reflected the vicar's keenness for evangelism.

Further building after the consecration was ruled out by the increasing demands of the war effort. The Metropolitan workshops were manufacturing munitions while the Great Central sidings were crammed with supplies destined for the battlefields of France and Belgium. Grassland was taken over for allotments as Neasden dug for victory; field crops were grown at the sewage farm and potatoes in St Catherine's churchyard. A 24-hour military guard was mounted at the power station, the vicar of Neasden served as a special constable and the need to rationalise services led to the closure of Neasden's post office in Kingsbury road. By 1917 Neasden had three 'rolls of honour' listing the names of serving parishioners and the fallen. The earliest was in the schoolyard at the corner of Quainton street; another, unveiled in May 1917 by Dorothy Nicol, was in St Catherine's churchyard; the third was on the site earmarked for the intended St Paul's church at Oxgate.

After February 1916 a Red Cross flag flew over Dollis hill house, signifying its conversion into a class A auxiliary military hospital attached to the Endell street military hospital near Soho and staffed by the 58th Middlesex St John's voluntary aid detachment, with Mrs Aubrey Richardson as commandant. A notable feature of the treatment here was the use of open-air wards.

Further towards Oxgate, on the crest of the Dollis hill ridge, St Andrew's hospital had been built in 1912 by the diocese of Westminster, using money donated by an anonymous Frenchwoman.[39] Put at the disposal of the Red Cross at the outbreak of war, it treated over 2,400 war casualties during 4½ years, including a number of Belgian soldiers who arrived in October 1914.

No direct use seems to have been made of Neasden House for war purposes, though the golf club actively supported the hospitals on Dollis hill. Part of the Grove, however, was used to accommodate convalescent soldiers under the care of the wife of George R. Glanfield, occupier of the house since 1913. Mrs Glanfield was also connected with St Andrew's hospital and she and other Neasden ladies like Mrs Collingridge at the Grange and Mrs Baird-Carter at Neasden Cottage were active in organising outings for the patients. George Glanfield and his brother Robert — both keen golfers — were partners in a clothing business founded by their father which had grown from a retail shop in the east end of London into a large-scale manufacturing concern. During the 1914–18 war they turned out millions of uniforms and greatcoats for the British army and in 1919 Robert, who had become president of the clothing manufacturers association, received a knighthood in recognition of the firm's services to the war effort. George, who was treasurer of an east-end hospital during the war, retained his interest in hospitals after moving in 1919 to Pinner, where he died in 1938, aged seventy seven. His son Dudley, who had grown up at the Grove, became a national figure when he defended his Surrey farm (on one occasion with a shotgun) against the incursions of the Electricity authorities in 1956 and a Ministry of Transport motorway in 1967.

B: *The North Circular*

When the war ended it was clear that Neasden's complete suburbanisation was not far off. A decade earlier, housing had swept over Dudden hill into the valley of the Slade brook. Industry too was slowly approaching. Already in 1914 British Thomson-Houston were in Neasden lane near London terrace and a pencil company (B.S. Cohen Ltd) occupied the triangle of ground bounded by Neasden lane, the Acton branch railway and the Metropolitan railway, whose tracks were doubled in 1914 by the addition of two tracks for fast trains on the north side of the station. In 1915 William Burton, the last of Neasden's old farmers, died at the stud farm, which was taken over in the following year by George Cloke, a cartage contractor from Kilburn who had won the contract for removing Willesden's house refuse for several years running in the Edwardian period, and again for 1916–17.

Down towards the Brent a major change was in the air. Motor vehicles had been allowed on the roads from near the turn of the century and they quickly multiplied. The maximum speed permitted by law, with tighter limits imposable locally, rose from a stately 14 m.p.h. at first to 20 m.p.h. in 1903, and the planners of Greater London soon realised that a new network of arterial roads was needed. In 1914 and 1915 the

Local Government Board in Whitehall held a series of conferences at which the local authorities concerned discussed what was needed and how this could be fitted into local development plans. For the north-western area one of the major projects was a ring road to be called the 'North Circular' road. Originating at the new Great West Road near Gunnersbury, it would run northwards along Hanger lane nearly to the river Brent at Alperton, whence it would follow the river upstream through north Willesden and so to Edmonton.

In a sense this was a road version of a cross-country rail project conceived in the 1880s which had come to nothing. While it lasted, the passenger service on the Acton branch line formed a kind of 'outer circle' railway for north-west London. But the Metropolitan had its own plans for an Outer Circle line to supplement the Inner Circle which already linked London's main-line termini. From a point midway between Ealing and Acton the new line was to run in a north-easterly direction to cross the Harrow road near Stonebridge whence, passing along the south face of Chalkhill and leaving St Andrew's church on its right, it would make for the Hyde on Edgware road and then for north Hendon and Tottenham. A minor feature of the plan was a short line to link the Midland's Acton branch line just north of Harrow road station with this new Outer Circle near Chalkhill, though there was a difference of opinion between the Metropolitan and Willesden's local board about whether this link line should pass under or over Dog lane. The first Outer Circle bill in 1882 was unsuccessful but Parliament approved a revised version put forward in 1888.

It is difficult to see how passenger traffic on this Outer Circle could possibly have paid its way. Fortunately, investors were more realistic than Parliament. The company were granted two extensions of time, in 1891 and 1893, but public support for the venture was so poor that when abandonment was sought and obtained in 1895 not a yard of land had been bought for its construction. The road project made better sense. Although it was recognised that such a road was perhaps not needed immediately, it was also argued that provision for it should be made forthwith so that it could be built without delay when the need eventually materialised; and because it would serve a regional and national need rather than a local one it should be financed mainly from national and county funds. The project was considered further at a later conference in 1916 but was then put aside until after the war.

Following the end of the war there was heavy unemployment because of demobilisation and the abrupt cessation of Government war contracts. At the same time roads were urgently needed. The war had started with cavalry and ended with tanks; and the principal user of main roads was no longer the trotting horse but the petrol-driven lorry. So road construction was given a high priority, leading to the Unemployment (Relief Works) Act of 1920, under which the Minister of Transport could authorise work to begin on road construction schemes before all the formalities of land acquisition had been completed.

The arterial roads programme for Greater London qualified under the 1920 Act but it was decided that the work on the North Circular Road (NCR) must be carried out in sections, sequentially, so that work could be stopped if the unemployment situation were to improve. In the 3-mile portion of the road lying within Willesden the work naturally fell into three sections because roads already existed (or had been delineated) in the middle section, whereas the two outer sections would have to be excavated across fields. The total width for the final road was set at 100 feet, including an 8-foot footway and an 8-foot grass verge on either side and two carriageways, each of 24 feet, separated by a 20-foot central reservation. But in the first phase of construction only one carriageway was to be built, the second to be added later when the volume of traffic required it.

On Willesden's western section, which ran for eight tenths of a mile over flat terrain from Harrow road to the former Dog lane, work began in December 1920. Much of this land had been acquired by Willesden Council by stages in connexion with the old sewage farm and there were already plans for a council house estate here with the names of Brentfield and Normansmead (after the old Norman's farm). Work started first, as laid down, on one 24-foot carriageway and one footway, giving employment to about sixty men at a time from the Labour Exchange. Willesden Council, which supervised the work on behalf of the county authorities, took care to spread the

Dog lane Neasden, before and after 1880

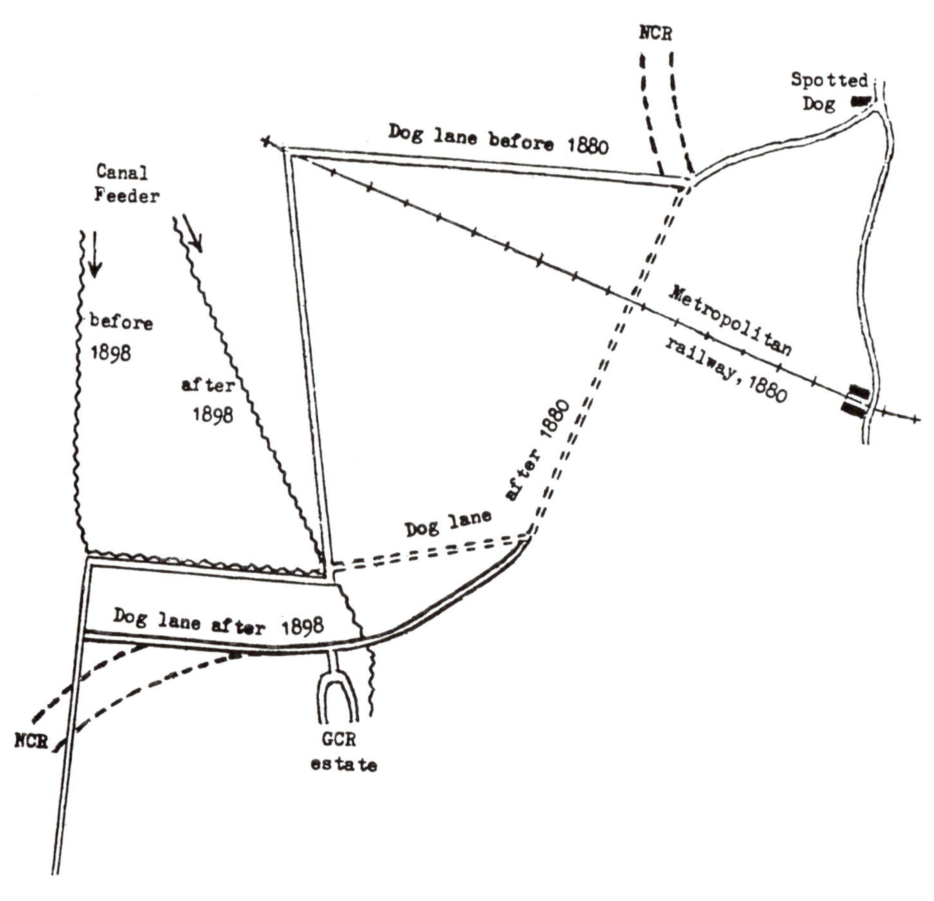

employment opportunities as widely as possible by engaging each man initially for a fortnight only, although about one in five got a second fortnight in the interests of continuity. This western section was opened for traffic in 1922.

On the eastern section, which ran for 1.2 miles over undulating country across the lower slopes of the Dollis hill ridge from Neasden lane to Edgware road, work started in January 1921. Because of the terrain, the labour requirement was relatively high and in the spring of 1921 there were jobs for a hundred and ninety men from the Labour Exchange, engaged on the same fortnightly basis as in the western section. This eastern section of the road was opened in 1923.

The story is different for the middle section. From the municipal hospital (the new name, from 1917, for the former 'isolation' hospital) to beyond the Metropolitan railway bridge the NCR was to take the line of Dog lane as established after 1898, apart from a smoothing away of the abrupt right-angle turn near the hospital. North of the railway bridge the road would use North Way on the railway's new 'garden village' estate, which was itself a pre-war idea.

C: The Completed Suburb

In 1912 the Metropolitan conceived the notion of forming an independent company to sell off to private builders plots of 'surplus' land near to stations like Willesden Green and Neasden. Plans were developed for a Neasden Estate, among others, during 1913; but everything had to be shelved when the war intervened. Unfortunately, when the idea was revived immediately after the war the Neasden Estate was wrongly described in a working paper as lying 'in the parish of Kingsbury' and the misleading title Kingsbury Garden Village was the result in railway advertisements, though the Middlesex county council sensibly stuck to the earlier name.

Neasden was recognised in 1919 as having been 'for some years past ripe for development' and a good profit was foreseen for Metropolitan Railway Country Estates Ltd from the land sales as well as more passengers for the trains. The estate would cover the forty acres enclosed by the Metropolitan railway, Aylesbury street, Neasden lane and the curving edge of the land purchased under the Act of 1873. It would have nearly four hundred semi-detached houses, with a few shops, roughly in the form of a square, with a pleasant garden-suburb character imparted by grass verges, curving green swards and a few quadrangles of open space. Within the estate three roads were to run northwards into Neasden lane, with two lateral roads, while a short new road parallel to Lansdowne grove would lead to the station. But there would be no direct access to Aylesbury street on the adjacent workers' estate.

Housebuilding had come to a full stop in the second half of the war with the result that when peace came there was a serious housing shortage, which successive Governments in their various ways were anxious to alleviate. Under an Act of 1919 the sort of houses envisaged for the garden village estate were given substantial subsidies. Building started at the station end in 1920 with semi-detached houses in North Way along the curving eastern edge of the estate, the houses on the west side being set well back near Village Way to allow a shallow green space at its mouth. But as time went by, some of the features of the original plan which were elegant but not essential had to be modified or omitted. For one thing, North Way had to be adjusted if it was to become part of the NCR and negotiations were still going on about this in 1923; for another, the plans of the Metropolitan for expanding the adjacent workers' estate called for some access thereto from Village Way. The result was that, although the grass verges were retained, the other open spaces were cut out and in the end there were more terraced houses (some in short terraces of only three houses) than semi-detached.

With the western section of the NCR from Stonebridge to the hospital completed it was not long before houses appeared beside it. In 1926 St Raphael's church was transplanted from the Great Central estate to Garden Way in the Brentfield Estate where it was the centre of an almost autonomous parochial district. Known as 'St Raphael's Neasden', it was run from 1940 to 1958 in close conjunction with St Catherine's.

In Neasden Village, as the Metropolitan workers' estate was known locally, the Metropolitan talked in 1919 of wanting another hundred houses for its employees but a few years later this estimate had shrunk to fifty or sixty. However, the new subsidies introduced in 1923 and 1924 for new working-class houses changed the economics of housebuilding and persuaded the Metropolitan to raise its sights dramatically. In the next two years Neasden Village was almost doubled by extending the three existing streets and building Chesham street along the bottom to link up with Village Way. In the construction of these houses, and of some in the garden village, use was made of the pre-fabricated concrete techniques developed during the war and employed for instance at Wembley stadium.

During and since the Edwardian period the Neasden villagers had developed their community organisation to good effect. In 1911, for instance, they sent a deputation to contest the Metropolitan's plan to increase rents by nearly twenty per cent. Arguing that the workers were on short time, that the company had no problem of bad debts and that prices in the Kingsbury road shops were higher than elsewhere in Willesden, the deputation succeeded in restricting the increase to under ten per cent. At the end of the war the Neasden Village Welfare Association was formed and on three acres of land obtained from the Metropolitan for a nominal rent a village hall was erected by spare-time labour in 1922. The site lay between the canal feeder and the river, on ground unsuitable for housing. After the expansion of the estate some years later a second hall was put up and a playground laid out for the five hundred village children, furnished with swings, see-saws and a sandpit at the railway company's expense. One of the high spots of the year for the children was the summer outing, usually to Eastcote, for which free rail passes were provided by the company; the vicar of the parish was allowed free travel on the railway at all times.

An important event for postwar Neasden was the Empire Exhibition at Wembley park in 1924–25, designed to show off British and Empire achievements and to expand markets at home and abroad. In advance of the exhibition Wembley park station was rebuilt and the roads from Willesden through Neasden were transformed from lanes into modern highways. The widening of Dudden hill lane and Neasden lane cost nearly £60,000, of which some £12,000 was for widening Kingsbury bridge and the bridge over the Acton branch line, and when the chaos of roadmaking was at its peak funeral processions from Neasden Village had to make a long detour to get to St Andrew's churchyard just across the river. Of the millions who visited the exhibition some decided to move house into an attractive neighbourhood, still largely rural but also well served by railways into central London and by the no. 8 motorbus service recently extended from Willesden through Neasden to the exhibition grounds at Wembley.

It was after the exhibition that houses started appearing east of Neasden lane on both sides of the NCR. On the river side of the ringroad the Council built an estate of houses, with roads all beginning with the letter A and called, from 1930, the Nicol Estate after the former owners of the land. On the other side of the NCR R. Costain Ltd began constructing the Brentwater Estate of about a thousand houses on the north face of the Dollis hill ridge beyond the limits of the golf course, while the Council put up Braintcroft school at the corner of Warren and Links roads, facing the Welsh Harp. The school was officially opened in 1928 but although extra land for an extension was purchased behind the houses in Heather road a much larger school was needed in Neasden to cope with the vast number of children now needing education. So plans were made to build Neasden council school on the south side of Aboyne road not far from Neasden lane. In 1929 the new houses and flats were filling up so fast that temporary arrangements for schooling had to be made, pending completion of the new school. Most of the unaccommodated children in the Nicol Estate were 'bussed' to Bridge road school beyond Woodheyes road and for a time various local halls were also used. The new school, named after William of Wykeham who had been prebendary of Oxgate for a few months in 1361, was opened in 1930, bringing the total capacity of Neasden's schools to about 1,500 places; and behind it, on the NCR, the 608 bus service now ran, operating from Stonebridge to Highgate.

At the end of Aboyne road the Neasden recreation ground, with a pavilion, was formed on twenty acres of ground, of which four acres were donated by Costain in 1928 and the remainder purchased by the Council with the assistance of the county council and the National Playing Fields Association. There was a brisk demand for its football pitches, Neasden Village Welfare Association being one of eight organisations renting pitches in the first winter. About the same time it was decided that, as the public library available for evening use in Braintcroft school was proving so popular, a full-time library for Neasden should be built on the edge of the recreation ground at the corner of Aboyne road and the NCR. Opened in 1931, it had the usual separate reading-room for newspapers and periodicals in the east wing downstairs and, unusually, had an open-air reading area for the public on the flat roof, with a splendid view of the Welsh Harp.

For almost all of the 1920s the old centre of Neasden remained unaffected by the changes taking place down towards the river. The golf club continued to flourish, taking now a greater interest in the welfare of its young caddies, which had always been something of a problem. C.T. Hill, one-time captain of the club, spent a lot of energy and money on the boy scout movement in Neasden, especially the 3rd Neasden (Caddie) boy scouts, in which that keen golfer the Prince of Wales took a particular interest when he visited a scout rally at Wembley.

The first scout troop in Neasden was formed in 1910, apparently in the GCR estate under the inspiration of the Rev. Digby, but large-scale events were normally held in the Dudden hill schools. A second troop came later, apparently on Dudden hill, and finally a third (caddie) troop at the golf club. The idea of 'caddie' boy scouts may have originated from Prince Arthur of Connaught, the grandson of Queen Victoria. It is not clear how often the prince visited Neasden in his capacity as president of Neasden golf club but when the foundation stone of St Catherine's church was laid in 1915 his telegraph message from GHQ France spoke of the church as being near to the spot where he had 'enjoyed much healthy recreation'. Prince Arthur also became in 1913 the first president of the boy scout movement in Britain; so he constituted at Neasden a link between the worlds of golf and scouting.

One way of raising money for the scouts was the holding of concerts at which members of the 500-strong golf club connected professionally with music and entertainment gave their services. One such concert held in 1922 at the Gibbons-road school had a long list of top-quality professional artistes including Ben Davies, the famous Welsh tenor who lived in West Hampstead, Harold Craxton the Queen's hall accompanist (from St John's Wood), Eric Blore (also St John's Wood) from the west-end stage, and Jessie Broughton (Cricklewood) from the world of light entertainment and musical comedy.

Besides its three troops of scouts Neasden also had a company of girl guides led at one period by Mrs Ayerst (the vicar's wife) as captain, assisted by Linda Potter (sister of Simeon) as lieutenant. As residents of Denzil road, the Potters would naturally have identified themselves with Neasden but Simeon (b. 1898) seems to have had no direct involvement with Neasden activities. After attending Dudden hill school he went on to Kilburn grammar school, the Navy during the 1914 war, and the university after it. While teaching at Harrow and before acquiring an international reputation in linguistics, he wrote a popular *Story of Willesden* with the elementary school children primarily in mind, which was widely used as a textbook in Willesden schools.

Between the wars, and indeed until 1954, the west end of St Catherine's church remained unfinished, the nave being temporarily closed off by sheets of corrugated iron which rattled in the wind and distracted the congregation during the services. In 1923 Ayerst left the parish, after completing twenty five years of devoted service, to become vicar of St Mary Bredin's Canterbury, and when he died in 1931 his funeral service was held in the cathedral. One of the tasks bequeathed to his successor at Neasden, the Rev. E.G.A. Dunn, brother of the vicar of All Souls Harlesden, was the building of the temporary church of St Paul's in Oxgate gardens which had been planned before the war and was opened in 1924. Another was the raising of about £8,000 to build a Memorial Hall next to St Catherine's in memory of the fallen. As with the church, the Nicol family gave the site, Dorothy Nicol cut the first sod and Randall Nicol laid the foundation stone. The hall was opened in May 1928 by Lady Pentland DBE, deputising for her father the Earl of Aberdeen, but it was still only two-thirds finished and its splendid west end was never built. In her speech at the opening ceremony Lady Pentland recalled how as a young girl at Dollis hill house, when she was Marjorie Gordon, she had had schooling for a time at a house in Neasden (presumably Miss Cuttrie's establishment).

With the development of Neasden now in full swing the golf course had no chance of survival. By 1926 the builders had already taken a thin slice of it and in 1929 the contents of the clubhouse were auctioned off. Soon afterwards in 1930 the rear part of Neasden House was demolished to make way for Cairnfield avenue while the front part was converted into flats, with rents of upwards of £140 a year, under the name of Neasden Court. Within a year, the houses of the 'Dollis park' estate, whose longest road Randall avenue was named after R.J. Nicol, covered the old golf course to its eastern boundary at Vincent gardens.

Further down Neasden lane the forge disappeared and the 1907 church hall had to come down to make way for the new 'shopping centre'. On the other side of the road the Wesleyan Methodist mission church which had stood since 1905 between Verney street and Aylesbury street was moved in 1928 to the south corner of the junction of Neasden lane with the NCR, on the edge of the land acquired by the Metropolitan railway half a century earlier. Although the structure had been designed to be movable, an attempt to move it bodily up the hill to the new site near the end of March 1928 failed when it came to a stop in the middle of the road. There it stuck immovable for several days while the police became ever more insistent that the road must be cleared before the England-v-Scotland international soccer match at Wembley on the coming Saturday. When Friday arrived with the obstacle as firmly stuck as ever, there was clearly no alternative to demolishing the structure and reassembling it later. In the meantime the Scottish eleven, immortalised in history as 'the Wembley wizards', had done their own demolition job on the old enemy with a comprehensive 5–1 victory on 31st March 1928.

Ironically, it was decided in the following year to replace the old wooden structure with a school-chapel in red brick and white stone at a cost of over £5,000. The foundation stone was laid in May 1929 and services began in the following October. A further irony was that the new building was to have a life of only eight years. Soon after it was built the NCR was developed, according to plan, into a dual carriageway with a diamond-shaped roundabout at the junction with Neasden lane and became so noisy that the Methodists gladly seized an opportunity to purchase 'the vicarage site' further down Neasden lane, building there a large brick church on the ground earmarked in the 1880s for Neasden's new parish church.

At Elmsted, as George Cloke called the stud farm after his arrival in 1916, much of the land was used after the war for sports of various kinds with Cloke himself acting as secretary for several clubs. For the greater part of the 1920s he had the refuse disposal contract for Hampstead borough council, as well as doing other work for them, and was allowed to put up, on the wall of an outbuilding facing Neasden green, three iron bosses carrying the NON SIBI SED TOTI motto of Hampstead across the centre. But it is doubtful if anyone apart from the firm's own employees was ever aware of Neasden's one and only public display of Latin. It seems likely, given that Cloke's wife was a Jackman, that the three bosses were made from a simple mould at Neasden forge.

In the early 1930s Neasden's shopping centre was completed after Elmsted park estate, lying between Neasden lane, Dog lane and the NCR, was built on, with roads named Ballogie, Balnacraig and Midstrath after the Nicol estates in Aberdeenshire. Although the whole of Dog lane had officially been renamed Brentfield road in 1919 Neasden people were so persistent in calling the eastern end between the NCR and the

'Spotted Dog' by its old name that in 1935 the Council decided to come into line with popular sentiment and 'Dog lane' was reinstated. Later, the no. 16 bus from Victoria via Crest road (a route inaugurated in 1936–37 as no. 92) used to run down Ballogie avenue to get to its Neasden terminus outside the 'Spotted Dog' until continuous complaints from the residents forced it to use the NCR instead.

In the shopping centre itself, midway between Ballogie and Balnacraig avenues, the Ritz cinema was opened in March 1935 with a seating capacity of nearly two thousand and was to remain for the next thirty years the cultural centre of Neasden, the other main contributors to the 'night life' of the place being the 'Spotted Dog' and the billiard hall over Burton's shop at the corner of Ballogie avenue.

At the junction of Neasden lane and Dudden hill lane, Neasden green, which had been getting smaller and smaller as the roads were widened, disappeared when Neasden lane was bent back so as meet Dudden hill lane at right angles exactly opposite to the new Tanfield avenue which ran past the double-bayed front of Neasden House. Directly facing Neasden House across Tanfield avenue a new vicarage was built for St Catherine's when it became the parish church of Neasden-cum-Kingsbury (population now 20,000) in May 1932, in place of old St Andrew's across the river. Two months later the part of the parish lying north of West Way, Aboyne road and the NCR became a separate district and new St Andrew's church, transplanted stone by stone from Wells street, Marylebone, was consecrated as its parish church in October 1934. A second reduction in the area of Neasden-cum-Kingsbury parish came when the new St Paul's, Oxgate, with its entrance overlooking Dollis hill lane, became a parish church in 1939.

One of the last green areas to disappear from Neasden was Gravel Pit farm on the south side of the river between Neasden lane and the Welsh Harp, with its access road directly opposite Verney street. For centuries gravel had been dug from the river bank both upstream and downstream of Kingsbury bridge and the part of the farm bordering the river was known as 'gravel pit fields' when Richard Freelove (d. 1776) was the owner. The farm did not belong to a local landowner until Prout bought it in 1881 a few months before he died. James Brailey, who occupied it for about twenty years from the mid-1880s, was known as a pigman; in 1907 it had the last registered sheepdog in Willesden; and it was still a cattle farm in January 1927 when there was an outbreak of foot-and-mouth disease. Half a century later people in Neasden Village with long memories still vividly remembered the air being filled for several days with the smoke and stench of the burning carcases. In 1928 the Nicol family sold the farm, on which Braemar avenue (another reminder of the Scottish Nicol family) was built in 1935–36 while factories occupied the ground between the feeder and the river and between Braemar avenue and Aboyne road.

Another large stretch of green, the 'broad field' south of Dollis hill lane, which had been used latterly as playingfields by Smith's Ltd, was sold in the early 1930s to builders including one called Lennox after whose family at least one and possibly three of the roads were named. On the other side of Dudden hill lane the Grove house lasted until 1937, its tennis courts being used by Neasden tennis club. In Dog lane the name 'Model farm' survived until 1935 when the buildings were converted into a group of commercial premises under the name of 'Model market', later replaced by flats.

It was, however, fitting that almost the final act in the transformation of Neasden from a hamlet to a built-up suburb should be the demolition in 1938 of the remainder of Neasden House and its replacement by four blocks of flats called Clifford Court after the man who was honorary secretary of the golf club at its beginning in 1893 and for over twenty years thereafter.

The Neasden which was to face the 1939 war and the world after 1945 had become just another suburb of London, as ordinary and to the casual visitor as undistinguished as most of the rest.

Appendix I

Neasden and Parliament

1. Sir William Roberts (1604–1662), owner and occupier of Neasden House, sat in:
   a. the Little ('Barebones') Parliament of 1653;
   b. the Parliament of 1654;
   c. the Parliament of 1656;
   d. the Upper House, 1658–59 (as 'Lord' Roberts).
2. Sir William Roberts, the first baronet (1638–1688), owner and occupier of Neasden House, sat as one of the two members for Middlesex in the three short parliaments in the reign of Charles II, i.e. in:
   a. the first Exclusion Parliament, March - July 1679;
   b. the second Exclusion Parliament, Sept 1679 - January 1681;
   c. the Oxford Parliament, March 21–28 1681 (in this parliament the Commons met in the Convocation House and the Lords in the Geometry School; rooms in some of the colleges were vacated to provide lodgings for Members and for the Court).
3. Baron George Carpenter (1657–1732), owner and part-time occupier of the Grove, Neasden, sat as one of the two members for:
   a. Whitchurch (Hants) 1715-22 (the first of the 7-year parliaments under the Septennial Act of 1716);
   b. Westminster 1722-27 (after disqualification of the Members originally elected).

Appendix II

The Neasden Prebend in St Paul's cathedral

Although it may not be true, as an ancient document claims, that king Athelstan in the 10th century gave lands at Neasden to the monks of St Paul's, the cathedral's connexion with Neasden undoubtedly goes back beyond 1,000 AD, and there was a manor of Neasden in the reign of Edward IV.

Near the end of the reign of James I, Neasden prebend was leased to Francis Roberts of Neasden by prebendary Thomas Wilson for a period of 21 years; and in 1649, when the parliamentary commissioners made their valuation surveys of church lands, Sir William Roberts held the lease as his grandfather's heir. Two years later, in pursuit of the aim of abolishing deans, chapters, canons, prebends and the like, the Neasden prebend was sold to the sitting tenant. Exactly what happened after the restoration of the monarchy in 1660 is not clear but we find the Neasden prebendary granting a 15-year lease to Sir William Roberts (the second baronet) in 1690.

In the long line of Neasden prebendaries the most famous names are those of the hon. Gerald Valerian Wellesley, brother of the Duke of Wellington, who was prebendary from 1809 to 1827, and canon Sydney Smith, founder-editor of the *Edinburgh Review*, who held the office from 1831 to 1845.

Locally, however, the best-known of the Neasden prebendaries was William Hawkins, vicar of St Mary's Willesden from 1699 to 1736, who was also rector of St Andrew's Kingsbury and of St Peter-ad-vincula in the Tower of London. Hawkins married in 1703 Mary Roberts, one of the 'five sisters' among whom the Roberts inheritance was divided after 1700. A good Latinist, he either culled from a Roman poet or wrote himself the half-line of Latin verse inscribed above the sundial (1732) on the tower of St Mary's church ('Dum spectas fugio'). He was almost certainly the author of the elegant piece of Latin prose on his wife's tombstone which lies at the threshold of the sanctuary. Hawkins also had the tenancy of the Westminster Abbey land at Neasden, which stayed in his family until early in the 19th century.

In St Paul's cathedral the 'Nesden' stall is situated on the north side of the choir and carries the words DOMINE NE IN FURORE – the opening words of Psalm 6. The psalms for the Neasden stall are nos. 6–11, being the psalms to be read on the First Evening and Second Morning of the month.

Appendix III

The Neasden House Charities

a. Lists of Trustees ("ten of the most substantial men of the parish of Willesden")

Year	1624	1660	1688	1722
Nominators:	Francis Roberts	Sir William Roberts (*d.* 1662)	Sir William Roberts, bart. (*d.* 1698)	W. Hutchinson & T. Wilkinson
Nominees:	Field, W.	Bell, T.	Brittridge, S.	Ewer, J.
	Franklyn, E.	Finch, J.	Etheridge, T.	Franklyn, E.
	Hartwell, R.	Franklyn, J.	Franklyn, J. (sen.)	Hutchinson, W.
	Marsh, W.	Marsh, T.	Franklyn, J. (jun.)	Marsh, J.
	Pate, T. (jun.)	Pate, T.	Freelove, E.	Nicoll, T.
	Pawlett, E. (jun.)	Pawlett, J.	Marsh, J.	Wayman, R.
	Pawlett, J.	Plummer, J.	Plummer, J.	Wilkinson, T. (senior)
	Twyford, H.	Roberts, W.	Twyford, J.	Wilkinson, T. (junior)
	Twyford, R.	Shute, W.	Twyford, R.	
	Vincent, W.	Vincent, W.	Wingfield, R.	

Year	1767	1813	1834
Nominators:	Thomas Nicoll (senior)	The Vestry or John Nicoll	The Vestry
Nominees:	Finch, J of Harlsdon	Bailey, T.	The vicar
	Franklyn, E of Oxgate	Finch, J.	Buckley, J.
	Gibson, J of Brans	Finch, R.	Curtis, W.
	Haley, J of Kilburn	Hall, J.	Denew, J.
	Mencelin, I of Harlsdon	Nicoll, John	Hall, J.
	Nicoll, J of Neasdon	Nicoll, Jos (sen.)	Peters, J.
	Nicoll, T (jun.) of Neasdon	Nicoll, Jos. (jun.)	Sellon, W.
	Page, F of Dolley's hill	Nicoll, W.	Trotter, Sir C.
	Pope, F of Harlsdon	Sellon, W.	Tubbs, R.
	Weedon, W of Wilsdon	White, P.	West, G.

There was evidently a nomination at some date between 1688 and 1722 about which nothing is known except that W. Hutchinson and T. Wilkinson were the only surviving trustees in 1722; interpreting their mandate strictly, they nominated six more trustees, bringing the 1722 total to eight.

b. i. "An Account of the Eight pound which was disposed of by Sir William Roberts to the poor of the parish of Wilsdon being one whole year's rent for William Lawrence's house due att Lady Day anno Domini 1688, which Eight pound is a yearly gift procured by the grandfather of the said Sir William Roberts:-

	s d		*s d*		*s d*
Widdow Baker	15 0	Widdow How	5 0	Willi Wilson	7 6
Widdow Coleman	15 0	Widdow Burton	5 0	Willi Palmer	7 6
Widdow Harding	10 0	Tho Roberts	10 0	Tho Gage	5 0
Widdow Barber	10 0	Mary Straight	7 6	Edward Gage	5 0
Widdow Randall	5 0	Susan Cockman	15 0	Luke Buknam	7 6
Widdow Fletcher	5 0	Tho Coleman	5 0	Math Maresty	5 0
Widdow Barwick	5 0	Tho Mansfield	10 0		160 0

source: *Willesden poor-rate books*

ii. "An account of the 20 shillings which was sent to the Churchwardens by Sir William Roberts to be disposed of to the poor of the parish of Wilsdon, being half a year's rent due at Lady Day last past, anno Domini 1688:-

Widdow Finch 6s 6d; Tho Banks 6s 0d; Eliz Croft 5s 0d; Tho Gage 2s 6d."

source: *Willesden poor-rate books*

c. In the year 1887–88 the Charity Commissioners transmitted £10. 0. 4d, being the dividend from invested capital, to William Edward Nicol and Catherine Nicoll Lewis Nicol, trustees, for distribution among the poor of Willesden. Out of this sum, eight tons of coal were bought for £7. The cost of distributing coal tickets and the coal itself to eighty houses amounted to £2.13.0d. The account for 1887–88 was signed by C.N.L. Nicol, trustee.

source: *Misc MS 67, Grange Museum library*

Appendix IV

Alehouse Licences at Neasdon

1. It is recorded that in court proceedings in 1422 at Willesden (spelt variously Wyllesden, Wylisdone and Wilesdon) John Bruer, publican ('communis pandoxator') of Nesedon, was fined four pence because he broke assize ('fregit assizam'); perhaps he overcharged or gave short measure.

source: Guildhall library, MS 25122/1370 (St Paul's)

2. In the 18th century the licensing authorities required guarantees of good behaviour in each establishment from two guarantors who each had to pledge £10 as surety; they were often fellow-publicans in the same parish. Perhaps the detailed requirements in the 'recognizances' were not in practice closely observed but in theory they were exacting. For instance James Tomlinson of the 'Spotted Dog Neesdon' had to undertake in September 1812 that he would not

> 'have, permit or suffer any Playing at Cards, Dice, Tables, Bowls, or any other unlawful Game, or Games, in his House, Outhouse, Yard, Garden, or Backside; nor suffer any Person to become drunk, or remain there Tippling or Drinking contrary to Law, nor suffer any Disorder to be committed therein, but do maintain and keep good Order and Rule in the same, according to the Laws of this Realm... '

One of Tomlinson's guarantors in 1812 was William Twyford, parish clerk of Willesden; the other was Richard Dunster, brewer, of Chiswick.

source: Greater London Record Office, MRLV 12/481

Appendix V

Parish Dinners at the Spotted Dog, Neasdon

The following are examples of dinners served for Willesden Vestry at the 'Spotted Dog' Neasdon at various dates:-

Date: 13 January 1779
Host: Edward Davis

	s	d
Leg of Mutton 11¼ lb at 5d/lb	4	8
Pudding, bread, sauce etc	3	6
Beer and tobacco	2	10
Punch	10	0
	£1. 1. 0	

Date: 15 January 1794
Host: Francis Stevens
"Bill for Dinner at Coal Money"

	£	s	d
38 lb beef at 5d/1b		15	10
Bread Sauce		3	0
Beer & Tobacco etc		5	0
Plumb Puddings		5	0
Punch		15	0
Brandy & Water		2	0
	2	5	10
Giv the servant		1	2
	£2. 7. 0		

Date: 1815
Host: James Tomlinson
"Bill to William Nicoll"

	£	s	d
Buttock beef 33 lb	1	3	4½
Vedgatabs &c		4	0
5 Bowls punch	1	10	0
Tobbaco		2	0
6 Pots Beer		2	6
	£3. 1.10½		

source: Grange Museum library

Appendix VI

Voting at the Willesden Vestry

For most of the 19th century the principle of 'one man, one vote' did not in theory apply in the conduct of local affairs.

An Act for the Regulation of Parish Vestries passed in June 1818 laid it down that a vestryman with a rental of under £50 should have one vote, a man with £50 two votes, a man with £75 three votes, etc., subject to a maximum of six votes.

This 'plural voting' system was introduced following severe criticisms made of the earlier system by a parliamentary Select Committee under W.S. Bourne appointed to look at vestries in relation to the burdens falling on ratepayers. Cobbett bitterly attacked the new system but John Stuart Mill saw strong arguments in its favour. It meant that at Willesden vestry in 1825 Joseph Nicoll had six votes to cast, James Hall four.

In practice, vestry voting was usually by show of hands, ignoring the prescribed voting scales, but on serious issues when a formal poll had to be taken the legal requirements had to be observed. On several occasions the Willesden records show both the number of votes cast and the number of persons voting. For instance, on the question about the future of the parish church in 1847 the number of votes cast was one hundred and seventy but there were only sixty four voters – a vote/voter ratio of 2.7 to one. On another issue in 1847 the ratio was 3.1 to one and in a case in 1863 it was 3.2 to one. Such ratios indicate that better-off people attended the vestry much better than the poorer parishioners.

In 1834 the Report of the Royal Commission on the Poor Law declared in favour of plural voting and for the purpose of the Poor Law Amendment Act of 1834 owners got votes as well as occupiers. Indeed owners did better than occupiers because, while owners had votes on the same scale as in the 1818 Act for vestries, occupiers were restricted to two votes at £200 annual rental and three votes at £400 or more.

In the later Poor Law Amendment Act of 1844 the voting scales for both owners and occupiers were harmonised so that both got two votes at £50, three at £100, etc., reaching a maximum of six at £250. The voting scales under the Public Health Act of 1848 and the Local Government Act of 1858 were the same as in the 1844 Act, so that a wealthy man might dispose of as many as twelve votes, six as owner and six as occupier. It was on this basis that the polls were taken in 1872 and 1873 about whether Willesden should have a Local Board under the 1858 Act.

Ward elections for the Willesden Local Board in the early 1890s usually showed vote/voter ratios of about 1.3 to one. On issues like the proposal in 1901 to run tramcars in Willesden voting was in accordance with the Borough Funds Act of 1872, which had repeated the voting scales of the 1858 Local Government Act. In this case the vote/voter ratios were 1.14 to one among those favouring the trams but 1.32 among those against – a difference only to be expected since it was the poorer people of the urbanised south who were for the trams and the people of the agricultural north, who did not stand to benefit, against.

Plural voting ceased altogether early in the 20th century.

Appendix VII

Neasden's Railways (legislation)

The following are the Local Acts of Parliament under which Neasden's railways were mainly constructed:-

Acton branch line

Midland and South Western Junction Railway Act, 1864: Hendon - Acton line
Midland Railway (Additional Powers) Act, 1867: acquisition by the Midland
Midland Railway (Additional Powers) Act, 1871: Cricklewood south curve

Metropolitan line

Metropolitan & St John's Wood Railway Act, 1873:
Extension to Kingsbury/Neasden terminus
Kingsbury & Harrow Railway Act, 1874: Neasden - Harrow line

Great Central line

Manchester Sheffield & Lincolnshire Railway Act, 1893:
Extension to London via Harrow
Great Central Railway Act, 1898: Neasden - Northolt line.

Notes

1. Rev Daniel Lysons *Environs of London: Middlesex*, 1795 and 1811; Stowe MS 862 (British Library).
2. The origin of the name 'Catwoods' is a matter of dispute. Michael Roberts in 1544 spelt it 'Catt at woods' and 'Catt atwoodes'. Some say that it is derived from the name Attewoode, others that the woods in the area were infested with polecats. Frederick Hitchin-Kemp (FRHistS) of Hendon, noting in 1905 that there had been another Catwoods in the parish of Hendon overlooking the Brent near the Edgware road, suggested that it was so called because a path starting here had been cut through the woods for rolling felled tree trunks down to the river.
3. Several wrong statements about the Roberts family which appear in the *Dictionary of National Biography* (s.v. Roberts, William) seem to have been collected by Burke (*Extinct Baronetcies*, 1838) from the detailed pedigree presented by John Nichols in his *History and Antiquities of the County of Leicestershire* (1811) and from the short account of the life of Sir William Roberts included in Mark Noble's *Lives of the English Regicides* (1798). For instance, the true date of the birth of the twin boys is established as 1604 (not 1605) by the baptismal entry in the parish registers of St Stephen's Coleman street, which also show that their father died in 1611 (not 1610). The second of these mistakes, but not the first, is due to a misunderstanding of the pre-1752 dating system under which the 'year' started on Lady Day (25th March); dates within the period 1st January – 24th March could be referred to as (say) January 1610/11 or 161$\frac{0}{1}$ or simply 1610, so that an entry in a register or on a monumental stone which says 'January 1610' would mean for us January 1611. More seriously, the Roberts baronetcy was awarded in November 1661 not to Sir William Roberts (1604–1662) but to his son William (b. 1638). This is proved by the description of the recipient in the patent as 'armiger' (=esquire), not 'miles' (=knight). It is confirmed by the fact that the first Sir William in his will called himself 'knight' and his son 'baronet'; and his widow did likewise when she petitioned the Lord Chancellor about the will in November 1662.

   Finally, perhaps the worst error in the traditional account is the description of the last William Roberts (1673–1700) as knight and baronet when in fact he was neither. The truth about the Roberts baronetcy appears in Lysons and in G.E. Cokayne's *Complete Baronetage* (1903).
4. The sum was defined as what was needed to maintain thirty soldiers in Ireland for three years at 8d. a day; in the case of the Roberts baronetcy, created in 1661, the £1,095 was recorded as paid in 1676.
5. The lane called Bowre lane had started roughly along the line of the later Tanfield Avenue. After about one hundred yards it made a right-angle turn southwards and after a further one hundred yards another right-angle turn eastwards. Roberts made the lane start about one hundred yards further to the south and enclosed within his perimeter wall the square piece of land on which St Catherine's church and vicarage were later built.
6. As Francis Roberts died on 5th September 1631 the payments from his charity should have started three or four weeks later; payments from Sir William's charity were due to start at Lady Day 1661.
7. Entries in the St Mary's burial register suggest that, contrary to Sir William's assertion in 1660 that the original trustees were all dead, two or three were in fact still living. For lists of the trustees at various times see Appendix III.

8. At Ware Sir William Roberts retained several pieces of land when he sold the manor of Sawtres in 1638. Chauncy in his *Historical Antiquities of Hertfordshire* (1700) says that Sir William Roberts of Wilsdon, Middlesex, gave three almshouses in Mill lane for the habitation of three poor widows and the profit of three cows for their support, the widows paying yearly upon New Year's Day one pair of gloves apiece to Sir William and his heirs, and that he gave two other almshouses in the same lane for four poor people. Clutterbuck in his '*History and Antiquities of the County of Hertford*' (1827) says that six almshouses were given. Cussans (1870–73) adds that the almshouses were endowed with the profit from four acres of land called the Widows' Meads. If these writers are correct it is most unlikely that Sir William (d. 1662) tried to suppress his grandfather's charity at Willesden.
9. This triangular field had a short side fronting Neasden lane and two long sides coming to a point along the line of the later Denzil Road. Originally the income for the £2 charity had come from land purchased by Francis Roberts from a Mr Leonard of Watford, situated possibly between Duddinghill and Neasden.
10. So universal was the phrase 'hospital land' that for many years after their inception in 1780 the Land Tax Assessment lists wrongly amplified it as 'St Bartholomew's hospital' which adjoined Christ's hospital on its north side between Newgate street and West Smithfield.
11. Under an Act of 1678 a family had to pay a £5 penalty if they buried someone in fabrics not made from sheep's wool. A quarter of the £5 went to the king, a quarter to the informer (usually the family itself) and the remaining half to the poor of the parish. At Willesden, for instance, the overseers' accounts show that fifty shillings received from Samuel Breteridge for burying a daughter in linen in 1686 was distributed among sixteen poor people and that another fifty shillings was paid by the same man for another daughter in 1687.
12. The Willesden lands were listed in a schedule to a Private Act of Parliament, 1759.
13. The evidence for identifying Samuel Spindler of Neasdon with Samuel Spindler the goldsmith is slender but convincing:-
    (i) entries in the Willesden churchwardens' accounts show 'Mr Spindler' as an occupier [of the Grove] up to 1767 and 'Mrs Spindler' from 1769 to 1773, and certainly Samuel Spindler the goldsmith died in October 1768;
    (ii) one of the witnesses of the goldsmith's will was 'Ann Wight of Willesdown';
    (iii) Mary, the goldsmith's wife, left £100 in her will (1783) to the Rev Moses Wight, vicar of Willesden from 1764.
14. The channel for the feeder was still being excavated in 1811.
15. A detailed history of the Royal Mint can be found in Sir John Craig's *The Mint* (1953) but not all of the information given there about the moneyers is correct.
16. In his oath taken in February 1781 John Nicoll swore "not to reveal or discover to any person or persons whatsoever the new invention of rounding the monies or working the edges of them with letters or grainings or either of them directly or indirectly unless His Majesty, his heirs and successors shall otherwise command...".
    (PRO, Kew: MINT 1/13)
17. The Rt. Hon. Stephen Lushington: doctor of civil laws, fellow of All Souls College Oxford, judge of the Consistory Court and of Admiralty, chancellor of the dioceses of London and Rochester; commemorated in 'Lushington road Harlesden'.
18. The account of the court case given here is based on J.E.P. Robertson's *Reports of Cases argued and determined in the Ecclesiastical Courts at Doctors' Commons* (1850–53).

19. This is probably a mistake for the Royal Hospital, Chelsea, where John's younger brother Alexander Adam Prout was assistant surgeon.
20. *Willesden Chronicle*, 13th September 1929.
21. From H.R. Forster's *Stowe Catalogue priced and annotated* (1848) kindly brought to the author's notice by Mr Hugh Pagan, librarian of the Royal Numismatic Society.
22. 'Model' farms were fairly common on 19th century estates, their purpose being partly to explore farming problems and partly to demonstrate to the tenants how farming should be done (see G.E. Mingay's *The Victorian Countryside* (1981), vol. 1, pp. 214-226).
23. The Dudding hill footpath ran in a straight line from the eastern tip of the Three-Corner Field across All Souls College land to the summit of the hill.
24. Unfortunately the committee secretary F.A. Wood failed to preserve Prout's letters in the records except for short extracts, though he preserved others; so for some of Prout's views we have to rely on what Wood says about them.
25. The Rev. Prout died in 1909 on Speyside in his native Scotland; a photograph of him by C.L. Dodgson ('Lewis Carroll'), his colleague at Oxford, appears in C. Ford's *Lewis Carroll at Christ Church* (1974).
26. Dean Stanley *Life and Correspondence of Thomas Arnold, D.D.* (1844).
27. The station became officially Neasden-and-Kingsbury in 1910 and Neasden in 1932.
28. It was during Gladstone's period of residence at Dollis Hill in 1887 that a drawing with the punning caption "Dollies 'ill: Mr & Mrs Gladstone nursing the dollies of Dollis Hill" appeared in *Punch*.
29. Kingsbury bridge was probably one of the bridges falling in part within the care of the Neasden prebend in St Paul's cathedral when it was sold to Sir William Roberts (see p. 18).
30. See also F. Herrmann *Sotheby's* (1980), s.v. Fairless; a portrait of Beeforth by Henrietta Rae was catalogued at the Royal Academy in 1896.
31. W.J. Gordon *The Horse World of London* (1893).
32. The passengers in the phaeton were Mrs and Miss Lithgow of Marylebone; but the details of the accident given in the *Marylebone Mercury* differ substantially from those given in the *Willesden Chronicle* (20th November 1891).
33. William Burton, who had the lease of the stud farm from W.E. Nicol, had as his sub-tenant Matthew Farrer, who made the arrangement with South with the consent of the others.
34. For a detailed study of this railway see George Dow's 3-volume *Great Central Railway* (1959–65), especially vol. 2; also L.T.C. Rolt's *Making of a Railway* (1971).
35. About a thousand photographs of the railway and its workers, taken in the Edwardian period by S.W.A. Newton, are preserved in the Leicestershire Record Office at Leicester; copies of a few of them can be seen in the library of the Grange Museum, Neasden.
36. Mr J. Pollard of Neasden, quoted in the *Willesden Chronicle* (13th May 1955).
37. The statistics are from the Midland company's records at PRO, Kew (RAIL 491/672, 675).
38. See also D. Frith *My Dear Victorious Stod* (1970)
39. For a detailed study of its origins see K.J. Valentine *The Founding of St Andrew's Hospital, Dollis Hill* (1983).

HISTORICAL WALKS round NEASDEN

Walk A: The South-West (Station) Quarter

Anyone travelling to Neasden station from the direction of Kilburn leaves the train at a platform where, a century ago, people coming from the direction of Harrow used to alight. Along the opposite platform stand some of the old station buildings with their attractive ornamental brickwork. We leave the station by a booking hall reconstructed in the early 1970s, when the original superstructure including the old chimney stack was removed, and we come into Neasden Lane. Proceeding towards Neasden we pass the end of Lansdowne Grove, with its Victorian pillarbox, and then, as we climb the hill, a row of Victorian villas. Then comes the site of the Model Farm, now occupied by Berkeley Court, where the road still has a very pronounced bulge, though not as big as it was before the farm's Edwardian owner gave up a strip of his land to allow the bulge to be reduced. Opposite to us is Prout Grove, named after John Prout, the former owner of the land.

Crossing Dog Lane into the forecourt of 'The Old Spotted Dog' we stand where Neasden's alehouse has stood for over two centuries (from the mid-18th century to 1972 the freehold belonged to the Nicoll-Prout-Nicol family); but before it was rebuilt about fifty years ago the facade faced Dog Lane where the entrance and forecourt were. The small estate of houses further up Neasden lane, on the left, recently replaced the 'prefabs' put up there in the 1940s. Arriving at the edge of the roundabout we turn left past the health clinic and make another left turn into Balnacraig Avenue, Midstrath Road and Ballogie Avenue (roads named after the Nicol estates in Aberdeenshire) to get back to Dog Lane. A few steps up Dog Lane and we stand opposite a building called Lansdowne Gardens bearing a crown and the date 1897 (diamond jubilee year).

Approaching the North Circular Road we note the cut-away corners of the building line where Dog Lane ends, before crossing the great 'iron bridge' over the railway lines rebuilt in 1938. Past the bridge, on our left, stood formerly the engine sheds of the Great Central railway's London depot and on our right the railway's carriage sheds, damaged by a doodlebug in 1944 and demolished soon afterwards. The NCR, which hereabouts follows the line of the old Dog Lane as redrawn by the Metropolitan railway after its arrival in 1880 (and further adjusted by the Great Central after 1898), crosses the canal feeder (constructed in about 1811) just before Woodheyes Road; nearby note the Victorian pillarbox.

We are now at the housing estate constructed for the Great Central railway employees in 1898, with eight semi-detached houses in the NCR just past Woodheyes Road, eight semi-detached houses at the start of Woodheyes Road and a further one hundred and thirty eight terraced houses, of which sixty two were in Gresham Road (named after a family connected with the railway). We note no. 7 in Woodheyes Road, which was for many years a Co-op shop before being converted back to an ordinary house.

Before entering the GCR estate we may have time to walk westwards along the NCR to the traffic lights at the corner of Brentfield Road (formerly Dog Lane). Here is the entrance to Neasden Hospital, which started in the 1890s as Willesden's 'isolation' hospital. Between here and the river was the sewage farm for the northern part of Willesden, used for sewage disposal between 1887 and 1911.

Walking though the GCR estate along Woodheyes Road we pass on our right the ground where St Raphael's church stood before being transplanted to Garden Way in the 1920s. We then come into Bridge Road with its large school opened in 1915. After the bridge under the Acton branch railway line we are not far from St Mary's church, where many interesting reminders of Neasden's rich history still remain. Inside the church are brasses, marble stones and wall monuments for the Roberts family of Neasden (roughly 1400–1700 A.D.). In the churchyard is the large vault of the Hall family of the Grove, Neasden, near the perimeter wall, south-west from the church. Near the path to the south door of the church lies Joseph Twyford, one-time publican of Neasden's 'Spotted Dog'. Many members of the Nicoll family of Neasden House who died in the 19th century are buried in the 'Nicoll plot' which lies beneath us as we sit on the public seats outside the churchyard. Behind us, in the tower, is the clock donated by Catherine Prout of Neasden House in 1869. The tombstone for her eldest son Malcolm Nicol can be seen to the right of the path which goes round the north side of the church. For further details about St Mary's church see the booklet *The Parish Church of St Mary Willesden.*

Walking along Neasden Lane towards Neasden we pass Chancel House and come to two short terraces of houses and small shops formerly known as Lansdale Terrace (after a local man William Lansdale Morley) on our left and London Terrace, with an Edwardian pillarbox, on our right. London Terrace, the western part of Denzil Road and Kingsbury Crescent (between Denzil Road and the railway bridge) were built on land formerly called the Three-Cornered Field, which for centuries was linked to Neasden House. Proceeding along Denzil Road for a short distance we notice that the oldest, Victorian, houses stop at no. 34 and no. 59. On our left is Selbie Avenue, named after the former general manager of the Metropolitan railway; further on, at the corner of Brenthurst Road, is the Edwardian house where Simeon Potter lived as a boy with his parents and sister.

Returning to Neasden Lane, we pass under the Acton branch railway bridge, first built about 1868. Here, after an exceptionally heavy rainstorm, the road is still sometimes impassable for pedestrians when the volume of rainwater becomes too much for the sewers which collect water from the south face of the Dollis Hill ridge and the north face of the Brondesbury ridge and convey it along 'Neasden valley' towards the river Brent near the old sewage farm. We climb the embankment which carries Neasden Lane over the railway tracks, remembering that it was built around 1880 to replace the original Neasden Lane which had hereabouts run some way further east on the flat. In Edwardian days it was lined on the west side with a row of coal offices which remained in business for over fifty years; some have recently been brought back into use for other purposes. At the station itself are some small commercial premises, one of which recently reverted to its original function as a bookstall. A short row of small shops on the other (Neasden) side of the station disappeared in the late 1970s.

Walk B: The South-East (Dudden Hill) Quarter

For exploring the south-east of Neasden we can start at St Catherine's church at the corner of Dollis Hill Lane. The outside of the building shows clearly where the eastern two-thirds consecrated in 1916 ends and where the revised west end begins. Originally the architect, J.S. Alder, had designed a more grandiose west end with an embattled tower at the south-west corner from which there would have been a splendid view; but it was never built. The west end was closed with corrugated iron sheeting until the much simpler design by E.B. Glanfield, who had designed Neasden's Methodist church in the 1930s, was realised in 1954.

In the external brickwork beneath the east-end window is the foundation stone laid by R.J. Nicol in 1915. Inside the church we find many items of furniture donated by parishioners and others in 1916, including the pulpit, the lectern, the pews, the altar rail and the sedilia in the sanctuary. On the wall of the north aisle we see the tattered flag of Dollis Hill House military hospital (inaugurated in 1916) and on the wall of the south aisle a 1914–18 war memorial on which half the names belong to members of the former Neasden golf club, including two of its secretaries, H.F. Williams and R.A. Hill.

On the opposite corner of Dollis Hill Lane stand three large Edwardian houses built in the corner of a 'broad field' which used to cover eighteen acres. Descending Dudden Hill Lane we pass three roads all probably named after the family of Lennox, the builder of the estate. At the bottom we note the line of the Slade brook, now culverted, with a MWB sign in the grass. At the corner of Mulgrave Road is the house where the curate of the parish was the first tenant. Climbing the steep slope to the bridge spanning the Acton branch line, which still forms the parish boundary, we see inset in the pavement on either side of the bridge a demarcation stone dividing the territory of the old Midland Railway from that of the Willesden Local Board which preceded the UDC. From the bridge we can see what remains of Dudding Hill station, now private property.

Returning a short distance to Normanby Road we remind ourselves that these two roads Mulgrave and Normanby represented the letters M and N in an alphabetical road sequence starting with 'Aberdeen'. It was probably thought that, as these were the only two roads on the Dudden Hill estate within the Neasden-cum-Kingsbury parish, the two names should themselves be closely related; in fact they could scarcely be closer, since the Earl of Mulgrave was also the Duke of Normanby. The houses on this estate all feature the bedroom balconies and moulded woodwork so fashionable in Edwardian times. Coming to the eastern extremity of the roads we avert our eyes from the hideous bridge built over the railway line in 1913 in replacement of the former level crossing and we enter Gladstone Park, opened in May 1901, three years after Gladstone's death and four months after the death of Queen Victoria.

The western edge of the park follows fairly closely the former boundary between Finch territory (Dollis Hill) and Nicoll territory (Neasden). We follow this western edge up to Dollis Hill Lane, noting on the high ground on our right Dollis Hill House (1824–25) and the kidney-shaped swimming pool near the western exit from the park. On the path east of the pool we are standing roughly on the line of a very old lane known in the mid-19th century as Scotch Lane. Before the alterations made under the 1823 enclosure award there was a large triangle of open space between the north end of Scotch Lane and Dollis Hill Lane, on the north side of which there stood in 1840 Scotch House, replaced in 1860 by Scotch Cottages, which are still inhabited and in excellent order. As Scotch Lane was continued down to Sherrick Green by a lane running at the edge of 'Bowling Alley' field, the name could possibly be connected with the game of scotch.

Directly opposite the north-west corner of Gladstone Park is Homestead Park, which again marks the old boundary between Dollis Hill and Neasden. The Neasden lands which came up to this boundary in the 18th and 19th centuries formed Turner's farm and when Neasden golf course was constructed in 1893 it had exactly the same edge. We can follow it quite closely by walking up Randall Avenue (named after Randall J. Nicol, second son and heir of Catherine Nicol, *née* Prout), then along Vincent Gardens and down to Tanfield Avenue, on whose north side the boundary corresponded precisely with the end of the houses where the grounds of Braintcroft school begin. It should be noted that on its south side Tanfield Avenue (Neasden) has maisonettes whereas its continuation Crest Road has semi-detached houses. The Neasden boundary then turned along the back of the gardens on the north side of Tanfield Avenue; note the line of trees along the path which leads to the original Braintcroft school built facing Warren Road in 1928, just outside the golf course. A little further west, the Neasden boundary turned north along the backs of the houses on the east side of Randall Avenue.

As we walk westwards along Tanfield Avenue towards Neasden we can meditate on the curious origin of this name. It commemorates, in a strangely indirect manner, Sir Lawrence Tanfield, a member of parliament for Oxfordshire in the reign of Elizabeth I and chief baron of the exchequer under James I. In recognition of his legal eminence the Inner Temple named after him one of their residential courts previously called Bradshaw's Rents, renaming it Tanfield Court; and it was in Tanfield Court in the Inner Temple that John Nicoll resided, near his work at the Royal Mint, before moving back to Neasden House in 1804.

At the Neasden end of Tanfield Avenue we see on our right the four blocks of flats where the front part of Neasden House used to stand. In 1930 what remained of the house was converted into flats and when these were pulled down in 1938 the new flats were called Clifford Court after Stanley Clifford, founder-secretary of Neasden Golf Club. The club was accommodated in Neasden House from 1893 to 1929 and Clifford was secretary (later honorary secretary) from its foundation until the 1914 war, although by then he lived near Staines.

On the other side of the road the vicarage was built in about 1932, when St Catherine's replaced old St Andrew's as the parish church of Neasden-cum-Kingsbury. The Memorial Hall, next to the church, was built in 1927 in memory of the dead of the 1914–18 war. Its foundation stone in the west wall was laid by R.J. Nicol and the partly completed building was opened in 1928 by Lady Pentland, daughter of the Earl of Aberdeen, who had had some schooling in Neasden when her parents had the lease at Dollis Hill. But the western half of the building, which was to have had a sumptuous facade with an oriel window, was never completed, as the brickwork clearly shows.

Walk C: The North-East (Brentwater) Quarter

For our walk round the north-east quarter of Neasden, between Tanfield Avenue and the river, we can start at the bus bay in the Shopping Centre (a term already in use at Neasden fifty years ago). Almost opposite is Cairnfield Avenue which was built across the back of Neasden House in 1930. The road may take its name from the 'brick kiln field' which once lay here and its right-angle bend seems to follow an old field boundary. At the bottom, by way of Avondale Road and Kenwyn Drive, we get to the North Circular Road which we cross by bridge to Neasden recreation ground. If it is the spring bank holiday we can watch there the annual regatta of boats racing over the waters of the reservoir, long known as the Welsh Harp from an old public house of that name located on the Hendon side of the reservoir beside the Edgware Road.

At the former Neasden library, an elegant building constructed in 1931, we stand at the edge of an estate built at the same time by the Willesden UDC and known then as the Nicol Housing Estate, on which all the roads start with the letter A. Aboyne Road takes its name from a town on Deeside in Aberdeenshire, Attewood Avenue from a family called Attewoode who owned the site of Neasden House six or seven centuries ago, and Annesley Close possibly from the town of Annesley in Nottinghamshire which was the starting-point for the Great Central railway's 'Extension to London' via Neasden. In Aboyne Road we pass the front of Wykeham school, built about 1930 and named after William of Wykeham who was prebendary of Oxgate in St Paul's cathedral for a few months in 1361. The school suffered a direct hit from a German rocket in March 1945.

At Neasden Lane we turn left towards the North Circular Road and come to a row of shops built in the late 1920s. Opposite are the new flats built on the site where Neasden's new parish church was to have been built nearly a century ago. A vicarage was indeed built here in 1887 behind the intended church but the whole site was acquired in the mid-1930s for a new Methodist church; this church was damaged in the rocket attack of 1945 but was repaired and used until its demolition in 1980.

We reach the North Circular Road (NCR) at Jackman's Corner, named after a family of blacksmiths who later went into the newsagency business and had the corner shop (note Jackman Mews nearby). Note also that this pre-1930 corner of the old road intersection is not cut away like the other three corners, which were built so as to be in alignment with a diamond-shaped traffic roundabout, replaced by traffic lights in 1953. In the late 1950s the idea most favoured was to take the NCR by tunnel under the radial road (Neasden Lane) but in 1972 an underpass was built in parallel with Neasden Lane taking the radial road traffic under the NCR, which was made impassable to traffic in Neasden Lane.

Passing through the pedestrian subway under the NCR we emerge into Neasden Shopping Centre which dates from the early 1930s. Walking towards the bus bay we pass on our right, before Ballogie Avenue, the site of the former Methodist church (1929–37). On our left two stretches of shop frontage unsurmounted by flats (i.e. the former Co-op shops and Woolworth's) indicate the sites of the 1907 church hall and the old forge of Neasden with its cluster of four cottages. Opposite to Woolworth's now stands the new Neasden library on the site of the former Ritz cinema (1935). Just before the roundabout, a car park occupies ground on or near which stood Neasden Cottage, once the property of Westminster Abbey. On the roundabout itself, the parking space for the Grange Museum is where Neasden Lane ran, after it was realigned in about 1930 to face Tanfield Avenue at the road intersection. Almost opposite to the Grange was the entrance to the biggest farm in old Neasden, variously called Neasdon Farm, Newman's Farm, Burton's stud farm and, after 1916, Elmsted.

We can round off this walk by a visit to the Grange Museum, the local history centre for Brent, which occupies a building erected soon after 1700 A.D.

Walk D: The North-West ('Kingsbury') Quarter

For a look round the north-west quarter of Neasden it is useful to take a short bus ride to St Andrew's Kingsbury (Church Lane). The 'new' church was transplanted stone by stone from Wells Street, Marylebone, in 1933–34. The 'old' church was formerly the parish church of the parish of Neasden-cum-Kingsbury which was created in 1885 and which stretched from Wood Lane in the north to the Acton-branch railway line in the south. In the churchyard lie some notable Neasden people such as Catherine Nicol (*née* Prout), who lived at Neasden House 1853–73 with her aunt Elizabeth, who is buried beside her, George W. Twyford the popular publican of Neasden's 'Spotted Dog' (d. 1902) and Francis Tarsey, one-time schoolmistress at St Saviour's infant school in Quainton Street who served as clerk of the parish until her death in 1929 at the age of eighty nine.

Emerging from the churchyard into Old Church Lane we can turn left and reach Birchen Grove near Runbury Circle, from the bottom of which we get a distant and restricted glimpse of the downstream side of the dam across the Welsh Harp originally constructed in about 1835 – one of the finest sights in Willesden. At the end of Birchen Grove we come to Neasden Lane and cross the river Brent by a bridge whose central stone marks the old boundary between Willesden and Wembley. Unfortunately, the two names were chiselled away when German invasion was feared to be imminent in 1940 and have not been restored.

Past the bridge, part of the land on our right was equipped in the 1920s as a playground for the children of the railway estate while on another part of it two community halls were put up by the Neasden Village Welfare Association which represented the residents. One of these halls survived for half a century.

Crossing the canal feeder, constructed in about 1811, we arrive at the Metropolitan railway's Neasden estate. The first sixty houses in Quainton Street, the first forty in Verney Street and the ten house/shops in Neasden Lane North between the two were built in 1882. An empty triangular space on our right as we enter Quainton Street was where St Saviour's mission church/school stood from 1883 to 1945. On the opposite corner, at 'no. 1 Kingsbury road' (now 409 Neasden Lane North), the first vicar of Neasden-cum-Kingsbury lived until a new vicarage was built for him in 1887. Further down Quainton Street are terraced houses built in the 1920s.

Proceeding along Neasden Lane North we find that Verney Street is generally similar to Quainton Street but the older part of Aylesbury Street has bigger houses and dates from 1904, which is roughly when 'nos. 1–3 Kingsbury road' (409–405 Neasden Lane North) were converted into plain houses. Between Verney Street and Aylesbury Street modern blocks of flats occupy the ground where the Wesleyan chapel stood from 1905 to 1928. The flats are named 'Chalfont', after the station on the Metropolitan line, and 'Brill' after the place near Oxford which was the most westerly point it reached.

We go down Aylesbury Street and at the bottom turn right into Chesham Street. When we reach Quainton Street we see facing us two semi-detached houses built for the railway's supervisory staff in 1882. Turning left here, we come to Neasden High School whose playingfield is where the Metropolitan in 1872 intended to have its terminus; later the field was the site of the reservoir storing water for recycling at the power station which between 1905 and 1968 provided the electric power for the Metropolitan railway system.

Regaining Chesham Street we proceed along it until it changes to Village Way. The next road, West Way, is now the northern limit of Neasden-cum-Kingsbury parish, the Metropolitan workers' estate having been taken out of the parish when St Catherine's became the new parish church. It is ironic that the name of the parish is still officially Neasden-cum-Kingsbury although it has lost both southern Kingsbury and also the workers' estate which was the prime reason for its formation.

In Village Way we are in the Garden Village built in the 1920s by various private builders on plots of 'surplus land' sold off by the Metropolitan. Some of the original grass verges still remain but most of them are now overlaid with asphalt. Noticeable features of this estate, which extends from Village Way to Neasden Lane North and from West Way to the North Circular Road, are the frequent use of very short three-house terraces and the open grass space where Village Way joins the NCR, reflecting the original plan for a more spacious layout than was in the event achieved.

Turning southwards for a short distance along the NCR, we notice the dangerously abrupt twist in the road where it suddenly stops following the long sweeping curve of the land purchased by the Metropolitan in the 1870s (which itself followed old field boundaries) in order to cross the railway lines at right angles. We can now return to the Shopping Centre by following the NCR past Village Way, where stands a group of shops built for the Garden Village estate in the 1920s. Alternatively, we can pass under the NCR by the pedestrian subway at the start of the bridge and follow the NCR northwards past Dog Lane to the footbridge over the underpass near the east end of Ballogie Avenue.

INDEX

to Parts One to Six

(For individual railways see under 'Railways')

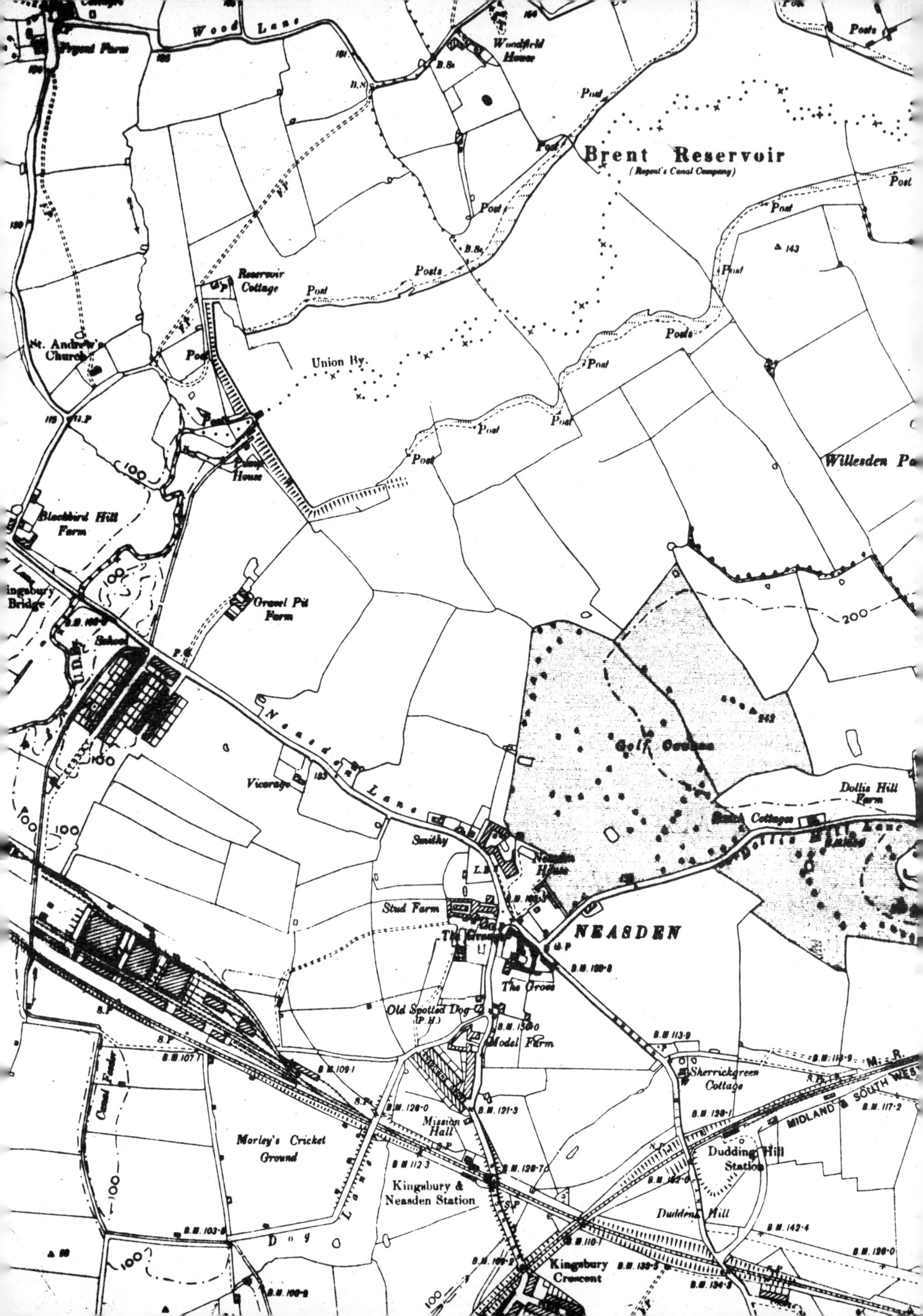

Wood Lane
Woodfield House
Brent Reservoir
(Regent's Canal Company)
Reservoir Cottage
St. Andrew's Church
Union By.
Pump House
Blackbird Hill Farm
Kingsbury Bridge
Gravel Pit Farm
School
Neasden Lane
Vicarage
Willesden Pa
Golf Course
Dollis Hill Farm
Dollis Hill Lane
Smithy
Neasden House
Stud Farm
The Grange
NEASDEN
The Grove
Old Spotted Dog (P.H.)
Model Farm
Sherrickgreen Cottage
Mission Hall
Morley's Cricket Ground
Kingsbury & Neasden Station
Dudding Hill Station
Dudden Hill
MIDLAND & SOUTH WEST
Dog Lane
Kingsbury Crescent
Canal Feeder